T0293518

VIDEO MARKETING LIKE A PRO

A Practical Guide to Creating and Publishing Videos That Convert

Clo Willaerts

Lannoo
Campus

D/2021/45/243 – ISBN 978 94 014 7792 5 – NUR 802

COVER DESIGN   Ines Cox
INTERIOR DESIGN   Banananas.net

LannooCampus Publishers is a subsidiary of Lannoo Publishers,
the book and multimedia division of Lannoo Publishers nv.

LannooCampus Publishers
Vaartkom 41 box 01.02   P.O. Box 23202
3000 Leuven   1100 DS Amsterdam
Belgium   Netherlands
www.lannoocampus.com

CONTENTS

INTRODUCTION

1.1 WHAT IS "VIDEO MARKETING LIKE A PRO"?

This book is a handbook for video producers who want to level up their video marketing skills:

1 **Amateur videographers** and even aspiring **online influencers** who want to learn the secrets of successful videos on platforms like YouTube or Tik-Tok.

2 **Marketing students** and content **professionals** who want to complement their expertise.

3 **Agencies** and other **startups** who want to take advantage of the higher demand for video-related services.

4 **Business managers** who want to get better at briefing and challenging their advertising agencies – or maybe even build their own video production team.

Video Marketing like a PRO is a handbook in what appears to have become the "Like a PRO" handbook series. I wrote *Digital Marketing like a PRO* in 2018. PRO is an acronym that stands for the three main parts in the handbook:

P for Prepare: strategy and planning. Hope is not a strategy! You need a vision and clear goals before you even start making videos. *Video Marketing like a PRO* will help you define an effective video marketing strategy, significantly increasing your chances of achieving video marketing success. If you want to make this strategy happen, you'll also need a plan.

R for Run: channels and tactics. Video marketing is the new content marketing. Before you decide which type of videos you're going to produce, you need to determine your content focus. A laser-sharp focus (or a niche, as some video producers like to call it) will help you stand out in a sea of videos. Learn about the broad spectrum of marketing videos that You can create, each with its specific purpose but with the ultimate goal to generate or increase revenue.

O for Optimize: anything digital can be measured and analyzed. As a video marketing pro, you owe it to yourself and your audience to constantly improve your working practices, personal efficiency, etc. If your videos fail to help you attain your personal, business, or marketing goals, come up with a new hypothesis and keep trying. Your work as a video marketing pro is never done.

It's not going to be easy. But what this book will help you with is not to waste any time, energy, and money, and instead, get things right the first time.

Let me know what you'd like to improve! Let's connect on Twitter or LinkedIn. Or leave a note on my website.

- twitter.com/bnox
- linkedin.com/in/clowillaerts
- clowillaerts.com

Reference to other chapters in the book

Want to know more?

Tip

1.2 WHY INVEST IN VIDEO MARKETING SKILLS NOW?

For the past 20 years, demand for video has grown across the board. For some of these video phenomena, the numbers are still baffling.

- Some videos "go viral" and attract a global audience of literally billions of people. For example: "Baby Shark" has amassed over eight billion views since 10-year-old Korean-American singer Hope Segoine uploaded it to YouTube in 2016.
- Livestreaming events attract more concurrent viewers than televised events do. Eight million viewers watched Felix Baumgartner's record skydive in 2012.
- Short-form videos have become very popular. For example, Zach King's Harry Potter Illusion has been seen by over 2 billion people on TikTok.
- For some, it is possible to make a living from their video audience. YouTuber Jeffree Star's net worth is estimated at $200 million.

Thanks to better connectivity, better screens, and better apps, billions of people can amuse themselves 24/7.

Then in March 2020, our world changed overnight. The consequences of the global pandemic were visible in reports about bandwidth usage.

- Video consumption went up 120% in 2020. (Wistia, 2020)[1]
- YouTube usage grew from 73% of U.S. adults in 2019 to 81% in 2021, with 95% of 18- to 29-year-olds using the service; 69% use Facebook and 21% use TikTok. (Pew, 2021)[2]

Video suddenly went from a "nice to have" to a way to:

- Cope with anxiety or escape a bad day. 80% of YouTube users say the platform makes them happy. (Google, 2021)[3]
- Pick up a new hobby or professional skill from the comfort of your own home. LinkedIn reported that in the first week of April, people watched 1.7 million hours of video content on LinkedIn Learning compared to 560,000 hours in the first week of January. (LinkedIn, 2020)[4]

- Learn from home when schools were off-limits for students. While video has been a powerful educational tool for years, 2020 has been a particular time for learning online. (Google, 2021)[5]
- Fight Zoom fatigue. According to Kaspersky's research, 37% of I.T. and cybersecurity practitioners watch videos on YouTube at work, while 34% watch films or T.V. series. (Kaspersky, 2020)[6]
- Compensate for social distancing with video calls and social media. In a March 31 survey by Business Insider Intelligence, 47.6% of U.S. adults had used Apple's pre-installed FaceTime app to chat with family and friends during the pandemic. Another 44.1% had used Facebook Messenger, followed by 31.5% for Zoom, 22.5% for Skype, and 18.4% for WhatsApp. (eMarketer, 2020)[7]
- During the lockdown, companies and brands had to change their marketing strategies practically overnight. Ad spending in the Video Advertising segment is projected to reach $37,418m in 2021 – a 12% growth compared to 2020. (Statista, 2021)[8]

In this unprecedented global moment, people are turning to digital video for more reasons than ever. Video streaming users across the world have watched content they probably would not have ever watched if not for the COVID-19 pandemic. (Facebook, 2020)[9]

As Google states in one of their consumer insights reports: "Need an at-home workout? An up-close-and-personal concert? A home-school sidekick? Digital video has you covered." (Google, 2021)[10]

But first: what *is* video marketing?

1.3 WHAT IS VIDEO MARKETING?

In 2013, American professor and author Dan Ariely was quoted saying that "Big data is like teenage sex: everyone talks about it, nobody really knows how to do it, everyone thinks everyone else is doing it, so everyone claims they are doing it."

Today, video marketing is like teenage sex. Many marketers know they should be using video strategically, but video is often just another box they want to check in their actual marketing plans.

The intent to invest more in video marketing is undoubtedly there. But in practice, marketers fail to see how using video efficiently helps them achieve their business goals.

Valuable video content should be at the core of your marketing. In that sense, our definition of video marketing is heavily inspired by the Content Marketing Institute's classic definition of content marketing. (Content Marketing Institute, 2016)[11]

Digital video marketing (video marketing in short) is a strategic content marketing approach focused on creating and promoting valuable, relevant, and consistent video content to attract, engage and convert a clearly defined audience of viewers and turn them into customers. Digital video is any content that is streamed over the web, including ad-supported and subscription streaming platforms. (Google, 2020)[12]

A good marketing video is a video that:

- your target audience wants to watch, and
- helps your organization reach its marketing and business goals.

How can you make good marketing videos?

By learning how to:

- attract and keep the target audience's attention,
- keep them coming back for more and even recommending it to their peers.

There is no fixed formula to produce this type of high-performing video. It takes time, resources, and energy. And most of all: creativity.

1.3.1 FIVE QUICK TIPS FOR MARKETING VIDEOS

1 **The key is to create a video that people actually want to watch.** That means something informative, helpful, or entertaining. It can't be a straight commercial because people don't like to watch commercials. It has to provide value to the viewer. (Miller, 2008)[13]

2 **Bring your story to life quickly** to instantly spark interest as people scroll through their feeds. In the opening seconds, you must clarify what your video is about and give the viewer confidence that what they're about to watch is worth their time. (Google, 2019)[14]

3 **Show, don't tell.** If your product or service offering is a complicated one, video is a fantastic vehicle to help explain what you do to potential customers. A well-thought-out video will show your service/product, its features, and the problems and challenges it will solve for your potential customers.

4 **Authenticity > perfection.** Authenticity (at least the semblance of it) is the glue that binds YouTubers and fans together more powerfully than the traditional relationship between Hollywood stars and their fans. (Stokel-Walker, 2018)[15] In "a world where consumers are more skeptical of ads than ever before, raw, un-overly edited videos of people using your brand in their everyday lives will bring in more new users than a commercial-type video." (Wiltshire, 2019)[16]

5 If you want videos that convert, incorporate **clear calls to action** that inspire a sense of urgency and direct users to an action that correlates with their purchase intent. (Google, 2019)[17]

HISTORY OF VIDEO MARKETING

It's safe to say that after 15 years in the trenches, video marketing has finally come into the spotlight. However, video marketing in itself is hardly new.

Video refers to moving images captured and recorded to project, share, and distribute to viewers. And although the oldest known images were created by cave dwellers about 50,000 years ago, the technology to project and share video is relatively recent.

The motion picture concept was first introduced to a mass audience through Thomas Edison's kinetoscope in 1891. But it wasn't until the Lumière brothers released the Cinématographe in 1895 that motion pictures were projected for audience viewing. (Saylor Academy, 2012)[18]

The first video track was recorded in 1927 by John Logie Baird. The word video was first used in the 1930s to describe the visual channel instead of the auditory channel in early television experiments. (Cassidy, 2003)[19]

The earliest examples of videos used to promote a business are found in the history of US T.V. stations.

1941 The first video commercial (for Bulova watches) ran on New York T.V. station WNBT during one of the Yankees games. In 1926 Bulova had also been the first brand to produce an advertising broadcast on radio.

1957 Start of the Marlboro Man campaign by the Leo Burnett agency. The ad was made to overcome the idea that filter cigarettes were for women and significantly increased sales of Marlboro cigarettes (300% in just two years!).

1964 The "Daisy" T.V. commercial for President Lyndon B. Johnson's re-election campaign. Ever since then, advertising agencies have sold presidential candidates as if they were cars or soap.

1971 "Hilltop – I'd Like to Buy the World a Coke" by McCann Erickson for Coca-Cola has consistently been voted one of the best T.V. ads of all time, and the sheet music for the catchy song that accompanied it continues to sell today.

1981 "Nothing comes between me and my Calvins" was a jeans commercial with the then 15-year-old Brooke Shields. Both ABC and CBS banned the overtly sexual ad.

1984 Apple's Super Bowl ad by the Chiat/Day agency is considered the best video ad of all time.

1993 "Wax" (or "the Discovery of Television Among the Bees") is the first film to be streamed on the Internet. In the same year, during a corporate event, Xerox tested their Internet broadcast technology by livestreaming the performance of a band called "Severe Tire Damage" to engineers who were in another room.

1996 The "Dancing Baby," a demo video created by a 3D character animation software development team, quickly "Ooga Chaka-ed" its way across Internet forums, websites, and email inboxes.

1999 The producers for the film "The Blair Witch Project" used Internet marketing to create the impression that the documentary-style horror film featured real found footage.

2001 - 2002 BMW ran "The Hire", a series of eight short films produced for the Internet. The shorts, starring Clive Owen as "the Driver," were directed by globally famous filmmakers and showcased the performance of various BMWs.

2005 Ronaldinho breaks the Internet with his "Touch of Gold" for Nike - the first online video to receive 1,000,000 views.

2006 The official birth of video marketing as we know it today. Google realizes the potential of video marketing and buys YouTube for $1.65 billion.

2006 Blendtec's first "Will It Blend?" video. Blendtec, claimed by its creator Tom Dickson to be the most powerful blender, is featured in a series of YouTube videos where numerous food and non-food items are used in the blender.

2007 "Battle at Kruger" and "Charlie Bit My Finger" are two notable examples of unique or cute videos made by regular people.

2008 Barack Obama's 2008 campaign features Obama's own words and a star-studded, upbeat music video created by the Black Eyed Peas' will.i.am.

2009 the Internet realizes YouTube is also great for archiving older videos, like Queen's epic "Bohemian Rhapsody" and Guns N' Roses hits "Sweet Child o' Mine" and "November Rain."

2010 When Old Spice's "The Man Your Man Could Smell Like" T.V. commercial was translated for the Internet, it became so popular that it led to a viral marketing campaign with Mustafa responding to various Internet comments in short follow-up YouTube videos.

2011 "Take This Lollipop" is an interactive short horror film and Facebook app, written and directed by Jason Zada, to personalize and underscore the dangers inherent in posting too much personal information about oneself on the Internet. Information gathered from a viewer's Facebook profile by the film's app, used once and then deleted, makes the film different for each viewer.

2012 "Dumb Ways to Die" was a Public Service Announcement by Metro Trains to keep Melbourne travelers safe.

2012 "Gangnam Style" breaks YouTube's view counter, making South Korean singer Psy the first person to reach one billion views, then two billion.

2013 Volvo Trucks wanted to show off the stability and precision of its Dynamic Steering, so it enlisted action star Jean-Claude Van Damme for a unique stunt.

2014 Polish YouTuber Sylwester Wardęga's pet dog Chica wears a large spider costume and becomes the "Mutant Giant Spider Dog."

2015 "Like a Girl" by Procter & Gamble brand Always smashes the patriarchy.

2016 The "Baby Shark Dance" by Korean children's entertainment company Pinkfong spawns numerous remixes, merchandise, and tours.

2017 "Despacito" by Luis Fonsi ft. Daddy Yankee and Ed Sheeran's "Shape of You" fight for the title of Most Viewed YouTube Video Of All Time. (Despacito wins.)

2018 "Bath Song" by CoComelon – Nursery Rhymes reaches more than 2.5 billion views on YouTube. In a market that's as saturated as children's content on YouTube, that's huge.

2019 Zach King's Harry Potter Illusion gets billions of views. (To this day, it is still TikTok's most viewed video ever).

2020 Spotify – originally an audio-only streaming platform - buys Joe Rogan's video podcast in an exclusive $100 million deal.

1.4 TRENDS IN VIDEO MARKETING

Video marketing trends help you appear intelligent at Zoom meetings and stay in line with consumer behavior and priorities and guide your business decisions. This way, you'll be able to listen and respond to changes in the market before everyone else does and save time, money, and resources.

1.4.1 THE GLOBAL APPETITE FOR VIDEO KEEPS GROWING

Everybody and their mother love watching videos online. Even though online video consumption has a long history, it has never been quite so ubiquitous.

The increasing popularity of online videos over traditional video content display methods shows in bandwidth usage. In 2018, the Cisco Visual Networking Index famously forecasted that by 2022 over 82% of Internet traffic would be online videos. (Cisco, 2018)[20] This number was 15 times higher than it was in 2017.

By 2019, the global average for video consumption per day stood at 84 minutes. The top countries were China and Sweden, whose populations spent 103 minutes per day watching online videos. The global average was expected to increase and hit 100 minutes per day by 2020. (Publicis Media, 2019)[21]

By 2020, in a typical Internet minute:

- millions of messages, emails, and texts are sent and read (Statista, 2020)[22]
- hundreds of thousands of pieces of content are consumed, scrolled, liked, and commented on (Statista, 2020)[23]
- an average of 16 hours of online video is being watched per week – a 52% increase over the last two years. (Wyzowl, 2020)[24]

Why do people enjoy watching videos so much?

Online video has become the key way for people to meet their information and entertainment needs.

Watching online videos plays an increasingly *personal* role in people's lives. Research by Google found that six out of ten people would rather watch online videos over television. (Google, 2020)[25] Why is this?

1   It's more **convenient**: now they can see what they want on their schedule.

2   Videos allow people to **connect on a more human level** than a faceless email or a more generic video. Video communication enables empathy. It will enable real people to tell real stories in ways that text or pictures simply can't.

3   According to Google, 70% of global viewers say that their **moods dictate their content choices**. "Many say they 'don't know how they'd get through life without it'." (Google, 2020)[26]

In some markets, online videos have even replaced watching T.V. as a daily routine.

Each platform attracts unique attention and interest. For example, audiences are more likely to turn to television for news and episodic content, to Instagram for beauty/style content, and to Facebook for animal/pet content. (Ipsos for Facebook for Business, 2021)[27]

How viewers typically watch video, across different platforms, on a weekly basis: (Ipsos for Facebook for Business, 2021)[28]

- 84% YouTube
- 81% Ad-supported T.V., e.g., YouTube T.V.
- 68% Facebook + Instagram
- 60% Netflix
- 39% Amazon Prime

YOUTUBE AND YOUTUBE T.V.

According to Comscore (Comscore, 2021)[29], the most popular online video property in the U.S. in 2021 is Google Sites, the owner of YouTube.com. YouTube has been the most popular online video platform for quite some years now.

In 2021, GWI (formerly known as GlobalWebIndex) moved YouTube out of the "social media network" category and into the "streaming service" category. When asked what prompted the move, the GWI research team replied: "We reviewed the social media questions last year and felt that the landscape had changed since they were first introduced in 2013 and that YouTube would now fit more comfortably into the T.V., film and video services." (Ignite Social Media, 2021)[30]

Read more about YouTube in Chapter 2.4.1

FACEBOOK VIDEO AND INSTAGRAM VIDEO

Uploading videos natively to Facebook had become a standard feature by 2014, seven years after Facebook was founded. Facebook's video marketing ambitions became apparent in 2017 when Mark Zuckerberg told investors: "We've talked about how video will continue to be a big focus and area of investment for us... The biggest trend that we see in consumer behavior is definitely video." (Stokel-Walker, 2018)[31]

Although Mark Zuckerberg's play for video still lags somewhat behind YouTube (Stokel-Walker, 2018)[32] Facebook users seem to be happy with the continued shift to video. Some 65% of Facebook users in the U.S. say they watch videos on Facebook every day, and 60% of people who watch online videos do it on Facebook. (AdEspresso, 2020)[33]

Read more about Facebook video in Chapter 2.4.7

Native video on Instagram was launched in 2014 and currently includes various video ad formats across Instagram Feed, Instagram Stories, and IGTV.

Read more about Instagram video in Chapter 2.4.6

On mobile, Facebook and Instagram's footprint is enormous. In the first quarter of 2021, the second and third most downloaded apps were Facebook and Instagram. (App Annie, 2021)[34]

The number one? TikTok, of course.

TIKTOK

Mobile-first and video-first app TikTok became a global phenomenon in 2020. When you add both Apple and Android downloads, TikTok surged ahead of all other apps in 2020, with global downloads of 850 million.

Today, TikTok's platform functions as "training wheels" for a whole new generation of future influencers and content creators. (Vaynerchuk, 2019)[35]

 Read more about TikTok in Chapter 2.4.2

NETFLIX

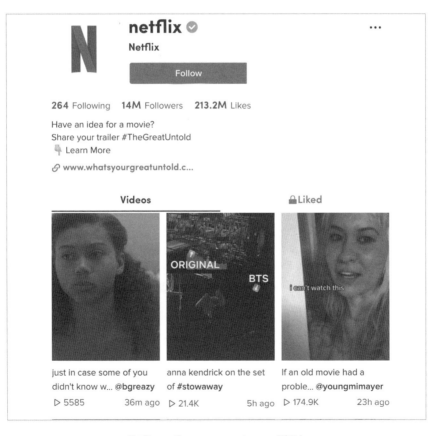

Netflix was the 2020-2021 winner on TikTok.

But let's not forget about the big video services winner of 2020-2021: Netflix. Netflix is an example of subscription video on demand (SVOD). With SVOD, subscribers pay a recurring fee (usually monthly or annually) to enjoy unlimited access to premium content as long as they continue to pay. It's one of the most profitable video monetization business models - and one of the most popular today.

In the U.S., more than 82% of video subscriptions fall to just five streaming services: Netflix, YouTube, Amazon Prime, Hulu, and Disney+. (Comscore, 2020)[36]

Even before the 2020 pandemic, streaming was already becoming the preferred way to enjoy content, pulling audiences away from traditional T.V. and toward streaming platforms. And while the rise of streaming was always expected (Google, 2020)[37] 2020 solidified this trend. (Google, 2020)[38] As a result, the industry experienced a livestreaming boom (Nielsen, 2021)[39] in a way that changed the media and advertising landscape forever. (Nielsen, 2020)[40]

And it's not all about YouTube or Netflix: in March 2020, Internet users streamed 1.1 billion hours of video content on **Twitch**. (Yahoo, 2020)[41] Shortly after that, the platform broke another record, with people watching three billion hours. (TechCrunch, 2020)[42]

 Read more about Twitch in Chapter 2.4.5

The livestreaming boom is far from over. For 2021, eMarketer projected that more than 106 million U.S. households would watch streaming content, eclipsing the number of households that pay for traditional T.V. services like cable or satellite. (eMarketer, 2021)[43]

People are generally interested in watching the same things: personalities, games, pop music, sport, entertainment, and humor. (Stokel-Walker, 2018)[44]

What do people watch online? A mix of:

- videos with high production value:
  - music videos, movie trailers, or video ads on video first platforms like You-Tube or TikTok, or on social media platforms like Facebook or LinkedIn
  - popular series on video subscription platforms like Netflix.

- user-generated videos.

1.4.2 USER-GENERATED CONTENT (UGC) IS STILL VERY POPULAR

Watching user-generated content has doubled over the past year to an average of four hours per week. YouTube dominates as the preferred platform for watching user-generated content (65%), followed by Facebook (16%). (Limelight, 2020)[45]

Fortunately, there's no shortage of content. Many regular people still upload their videos to YouTube, Facebook, TikTok, Twitch, and other social media platforms. Regardless of the platform, more and more videos are being created and published. In 2020, overall total video creation increased by 135%. (Vidyard, 2021)[46]

Every day brings a new series to watch, creator to follow, or trend to try. Digital video, including user generated content in video format, continues to meet our needs in new and compelling ways. (Facebook, 2020)[47]

User generated content (UGC) is any content - text, videos, images, reviews, etc. - created by people, rather than brands. (HootSuite, 2019)[48]

The watershed moment for user-generated video was the launch of YouTube in 2005 and its acquisition by Google the year after. Before YouTube, video was an elite, exclusive, and inaccessible content format, reserved for motion pictures, broadcast news, and other high-production programming that would be televised or shown in theaters. Video cameras, video editing technology, and video distribution processes were all prohibitively expensive and required specialized training to operate. (Deziel, 2020)[49]

Since the launch of Facebook in 2007, social media platforms like Facebook, Instagram, LinkedIn, Snapchat, and TikTok have further democratized creating and sharing user-generated videos.

In a U.K. consumer survey (Ofcom, 2019)[50], a variety of factors were considered necessary by users of Facebook, Twitter, Snapchat, Instagram, and YouTube:

* keeping in touch with friends and family
* browsing to pass the time
* sharing photos and videos
* keeping up-to-date with news and current affairs; and
* watching videos

Let's not forget the popularity of smartphones, either. A lot has changed since the launch of Steve Jobs' "one more thing," the iPhone, in 2007.

- Today most of us have a phone in our pockets that can perfectly capture decent quality videos.
- The Internet enables us to host and distribute video content without the need for a broadcast station license or a film studio's support.
- Video editing software has become cheaper and easier to use.

User-generated video creation increased 44% in the second quarter of the 2020 calendar year - aligning with the initial stages of the COVID-19 pandemic. (Vidyard, 2020)[51]

- 60% of all videos created in 2020 were user-generated or user recorded, representing an increase of 128% over user-generated content in 2019. (Vidyard, 2020)[52]
- Five hundred hours of video are uploaded to YouTube every minute worldwide. (Tubefilter, 2019)[53] And 83% of the estimated one billion TikTok users have posted at least one video. (Wallaroom, 2021)[54]

And it's not just regular people who upload videos! Approximately 75% of video content created by companies with under 200 employees is user generated, while 45% of the video content created by organizations with more than 600 employees is user generated. (Vidyard, 2020)[55]

 See Chapter 2.5 for an overview of the most notable video marketing platforms

MOBILE FIRST IS NOW THE NORM

Somewhere in the summer of 2016, mobile Internet usage surpassed desktop usage. (StatCounter, 2016)[56]

- According to Facebook, people are 1.5 times more likely to watch videos on their mobile devices. (Facebook, 2019)[57]
- In 2019, more than 70% of YouTube watch time came from mobile devices. (YouTube, 2019)[58]

Today, mobile is first everywhere. We're spending more time on our mobile phones than ever before.

- People spend on average three hours and 43 minutes per day staring at a cell phone screen. Throughout a lifetime, this amounts to almost nine years. (WhistleOut, 2020)[59]
- Global mobile video viewership is growing by 6% annually, outpacing growth on other video platforms. (eMarketer, 2019)[60]
- More than 60% of music consumption on YouTube happens on mobile devices (as of June 2020).[61]
- Mobile video consumption increases by 100% every year. (Vidyard, 2021)[62]
- Video currently accounts for 63% of mobile traffic. Based on smartphone analytics, Ericsson predicts a 25% increase in mobile traffic by 2025. (Ericsson, 2020)[63]
- App Annie predicts that by 2021 the average mobile streamer in the U.S., South Korea, and the U.K. will download 85%, 80%, and 60% more video streaming apps, respectively, compared to pre-pandemic levels. (App Annie, 2021)[64]
- Fifteen percent of adults and almost two in five (37%) 18-24-year-olds say they watch gameplay videos on services such as YouTube or Twitch every month. 56% of 8- to 15-year-olds say they watch game videos online. (Ofcom, 2020)[65]

This perfect storm was enabled by the convergence of eight contributing factors driving people to online video.

On the content demand side:

- Hunger for more videos to watch

On the technology side:

- More mobile Internet users and more mobile connections
- More and faster mobile devices with better screens and built-in cameras
- Faster, improved, and cheaper connectivity (broadband, 5G)
- More video streaming and sharing services

On the content production side:

- More and more video content available in web browsing and social media
- Easier to use video editing and publishing software and apps
- Cloud solutions to host and back up videos

VIDEO MARKETING IS THE NEW CONTENT MARKETING

Marketers are inundated with reports where consumers say that videos are their preferred content format.

- 90% of people claim they discover new brands or products on YouTube. (Google, 2019)[66]
- 68% of people say they'd like to learn about a new product or service by watching a short video. (Google, 2019)[67]
- Only a small percentage of respondents preferred text-based articles (15%), infographics (4%), presentations (4%), or ebooks/manuals (3%) for learning information. (Google, 2019)[68]
- Nearly three-quarters of millennials report that videos are helpful when they are comparing products during online shopping. (TechJury, 2020)[69]
- 82% of viewers say they prefer seeing a livestream rather than a brand's social posts. (Tech Jury, 2020)[70]
- 80% of people would rather watch a live video from a brand than read their blog. (Tech Jury, 2020)[71]
- 86% of people would like to see more videos from brands in 2020. (Wyzowl, 2020)[72]

This is not the only reason why marketing professionals have a sense of urgency. Video is a visual medium. 90% of information transmitted to the brain is visual, and visuals are processed 60,000 times faster in the brain than text. (Walter, 2014)[73]

The dual coding theory, created by Allan Paivio in 1971, suggests that presenting information verbally and non-verbally makes it easier to remember. (Design Psychology, 2018)[74] In theory, this implies that a media-rich format like video is more powerful than pictures or texts.

No wonder, then, that video marketing is flourishing on all social media platforms that support the medium, ranging from Facebook and LinkedIn to Twitter. Even Instagram has taken steps toward including videos on its platform in the form of Instagram Reels and IGTV.

Compared to other content formats, videos also get more engagement. One of the key ways social media platforms measure whether a piece of content resonates with their audience is engagement. Whether a viewer likes, comments on, or shares a post is more important than whether someone merely viewed it.

This is not even the main reason video marketing is so powerful. Video allows you to create a human connection with your audience while building trust.

Put bluntly, the only purpose of your organization's video presence is:

1   To get repeat traffic from your community, your tribe (e.g., subscribers to your channel), and

2   To build trust.

Don't forget it takes a lot of trust for someone to pull out their wallet and transfer money. That's a gigantic leap of faith – they only do it based on the belief that you will help them solve their problems.

In general, we all prefer to connect and do business with people we know, like, and trust. The problem with connecting online is that it's harder to look someone in the eye, have an honest conversation with them, and gauge their facial expressions. This is particularly true with blogging but also holds for audio content. That's one reason we believe video is absolutely the best way to communicate any message. (Cannell & Travis 2018)[75]

Know, Like, Trust

	KNOW	LIKE	TRUST
If what your audience sees in your videos …	is instantly recognizable through consistent branding	is relatable to their life	makes you appear trustworthy enough to risk a purchase
… they will …	recognize you	follow you	buy from you

Through video, it's much easier for an audience to get to know and trust you. The most successful YouTubers have regular viewers who feel like they have developed a friendship with them. Only video engages people on that level. (Cannell & Travis 2018)[76]

A famous example of this type of engagement is the YouTuber with the largest number of subscribers, PewDiePie. He is a Swedish guy called Felix Kjellberg, best known for his "Let's Play" videos. Millions of people worldwide tune in to his YouTube channel to watch him play video games like Minecraft. Kjellberg isn't necessarily the best in the world at playing those games. Viewers aren't watching them for tips on how to break down an opponent or to conquer a particularly tricky level. They want companionship and a sense of connection – an invitation into someone else's life and the ability to make a remote friend, albeit one mediated through a camera. What gamers do away from the keyboard matters as much as their dexterity with a gamepad. (Stokel-Walker, 2018)[77]

Some of PewDiePie's gaming videos have tens of millions of views.

It is a lot easier for a handsome young Swede to attract fans who want to be like him. What about organizations who want their audience to know, like, and trust them enough, so their videos lead to a growth in revenue?

How do you build awareness with video marketing?

 See also Chapter 4.1 for best practices to create awareness for your brand using videos

How do you build likability with video marketing?

By showing the human side of your organization.

Video is a powerful medium that allows you to create an emotional connection with your target audience by telling the story of your business and why you do what you do.

Behind-the-scenes videos are a great way to show what's going on at your company. They show the culture and employees and can build a great connection with your audience. It is perfect for Instagram or even LinkedIn Stories!

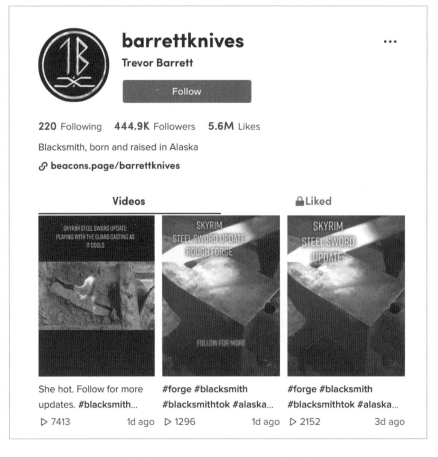

Barrett Knives on TikTok show a struggling company making a fantastic product.

Behind-the-scenes videos are an ideal way to make the business and staff more likable. Emphasize everyday tasks, workplaces, development processes, and more. Interview personnel, speak to your suppliers or talk to your best customers. Each of these things helps the viewer understand the way your business operates and reveals your identity. Such videos promote brand identity and help build trust. (Olson 2020)[78]

When we look at storytelling style, we see that emotional elements, such as action, intrigue, and surprise, work well across the funnel. (Google, 2019)[79]

Because of its visual nature, storytelling happens to be one of the most potent tactics in video marketing.

We are hardwired to respond to stories (Mowat, 2018)[80] that:

- Move: mobile video is made up of moving images, which our brain engages with more than still images or spoken words.
- Are held in our hand: we watch video on our mobile, a device to which we feel connected and on which we store much of our life. As we touch the screen, we feel more ownership of what we are looking at as we get physical feedback from our fingers, which drives psychological connections.

Telling stories that speak to audiences and meeting their communication styles and needs is one of the most important skills you can learn. (Kane, 2008)[81]

 Sharpen your video production skills in Chapter 3

What does this mean for the actual marketing budget spending? Marketing budgets, especially media budgets, are always first in line when budget cuts need to be made.

This was no different in 2020 when the economic repercussions of the global pandemic started to materialize. Research from IAB UK found that U.K. digital ad spend fell by 5% in H1 2020 compared with figures from the first half of 2019.

However, some advertising sub-categories were immune to the budget cuts.

- Nielsen saw a rise in digital game purchases, streaming video engagement and online ordering due to increased working at home during the peak pandemic months. Out of necessity, businesses quickly moved not just their workforces but their services and more of their advertising online. (Nielsen, 2021)[82]

- Display advertising grew by 0.3% year-on-year to £2.84 billion, within which video advertising rose 5.7%, mirroring increased engagement consumers had with video streaming services over lockdown. Without video's strong growth, overall digital ad spend results would have been much worse. (WARC, 2020)[83]
- In the year that followed, online video saw the largest net budget increase due to the coronavirus outbreak, and more practitioners are planning to increase spending in 2021. (WARC, 2020)[84]

Videos are not only a consumer favorite:

- 92% of marketers who use video say that it's an important part of their marketing strategy. (Up from 91% in 2019, 85% in 2018, 82% in 2017, 88% in 2016 and 78% in 2015.) (Wyzowl, 2020)[85]
- Social media, search, and video rank as the top channels companies will invest in over 2021, but they need to go beyond these channels to acquire and retain customers. (Nielsen, 2021)[86]
- In 2020, 92% of marketers said that video is an important part of their marketing strategy. According to 88% of marketers, video marketing provides them with positive ROI. (Smart Insights, 2020)[87]

Who uses video marketing? (Vidyard, 2020)[88]

- Organizations in high tech reign supreme when it comes to overall video creation and user-generated videos.
- If we look exclusively at produced or uploaded video, retail and consumer goods inch ahead.

The most common types of marketing videos are:

- how-to's, with a 50% increase on 2019 results (Vidyard, 2020)[89]
- product demos,
- explainers, and
- webinars.

Social media, websites, and YouTube are the most popular distribution channels for video content. (Vidyard, 2020)[90]

However, just as with teenagers and sex, there's a difference between what marketers say and what they do.

Animoto (2019)[91] found that marketers are unaware of their marketing strategies, and what they think they do differs vastly from what they are doing.

- Marketers know that video works and helps them gain the attention of many prospective customers.
- But they fail to create good video content since it's too time-consuming. Lack of resources is another reason that holds them back from achieving success with video.

1.4.5 THE DIGITAL VIDEO GOLD RUSH

The best time to invest in video marketing was 20 years ago. The second best time is now.

- The demand for more online videos is there.
- Mobile technologies enable exponential growth in both video production and consumption.
- Video marketing is slowly but surely becoming a staple of overall marketing strategies. From a business perspective, it's more important than ever to invest in video marketing. In a socially distanced world, video still allows people and companies to make human-to-human connections.
- Lower production costs, cheaper hardware, and software (smartphones!). A well-produced video campaign may seem expensive, but it's nothing like what it used to cost 20 years ago.
- Livestreaming alone is set to become a $70 billion industry by 2021. (P.R. Newswire, 2020)[92]

The market for digital video production is a hungry one.

In 2020, over half of small and medium companies moved towards using internal resources for video production. Most small and medium companies use internal resources exclusively to produce their video content, while large enterprises are more evenly split between internal, external, or both. (Vidyard, 2020)[93]

Video producer freelancers are in high demand, and they know what they're worth.

In its latest analysis of rising job categories in the UK, based on growth and size of demand, LinkedIn places digital marketing, digital content and social media marketing among the top 15 of 2021 by LinkedIn. Ranking below eCommerce and healthcare support staff, digital content freelancing came in at number three, growing 118% in 2020 due to the number of U.K. workers turning to freelance during the coronavirus outbreak. This includes podcasting, blogging, and video editing, with the most common job title being Content Coordinator. (LinkedIn, 2021)[94]

So as a business, you either challenge marketing agencies' hefty video content production fees or grow your video team.

Know your strengths and find people who can cover for you in weak areas, like video editing or creating videos that are optimized for social media. Another possibility: upskill to become your own Solo Video Production unit. Not only will this save you the costs, but you'll also be able to better brief any freelancers you can outsource part of the video creation process to.

At least 50% of your content should be video. Your audiences want to live inside video. Stop hiring bloggers; start hiring producers. (HubSpot CEO Brian Halligan)

The choice is yours.

1.4.6   VIDEOS ARE SOCIAL CURRENCY IN ONLINE COMMUNITIES

What is a community?

A community is a type of organization that brings people together and gives them a sense of belonging to a club of like-minded people. It provides a framework to trust each other more, support each other more, collaborate more, and build more meaningful relationships. (Willaerts, 2018)[95]

The sense of belonging to a club of like-minded people is crucial in all sorts of communities, both offline and online. Wanting to belong is a human need. In Maslow's Hierarchy of Needs, "love and belonging" comes third, right behind physiological needs (like food, water, sleep, and sex) and safety needs (like a stable environment). (McLeod, 2020)[96]

What do we mean by social currency? Even online communities need something to talk about to strengthen social ties and keep the conversation going. Very often, this is the equivalent of "small change" in financial currencies.

Casey Neistat's 165th vlog shows him watching his girlfriend interact with their infant daughter, going for a run, and mowing the lawn.

Vloggers like Casey Neistat can engage a large audience purely based on the relationship that the audience has with the creator. Although his audience would want him to, Neistat cannot pay back their attention in one-on-one conversations. He pays them back in vlogs: short videos about these daily activities. The relationship with his audience is that they'll essentially watch that creator do anything, like drinking coffee or mowing the lawn.

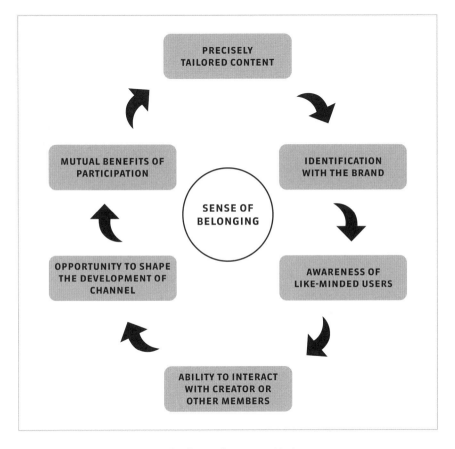

What drives online communities?

1   Identification with the brand

The simplest form of community unites fans of a particular brand, organization, or person.

LEGO's YouTube channel is one of the most popular brand channels with well over 10 million subscribers.

Communities can also form around shared life stages or activities. Sometimes the activity is impossible to do alone. Other times the activity is fine solo but 10 times better when done with others. (Richardson, Sotto & Huynh, 2019)[97]

2   Awareness of like-minded users

The awareness of like-minded users is key to the success of Twitch.tv. Twitch rallies video gamers, so they don't have to game alone.

3   Ability to interact with others on the platform

- With the video creator
- With other viewers

There are quite a few creators who use public video as a "top of the funnel" and then use that to pull people into private communities with access to livestreams, hidden videos, chat… Patreon is often used for this, with unique videos for patrons that remain exclusive to them. Telegram groups are often promoted as a way to gather a sort of in-crowd. Twitch subscribers tend to get access to special emotes and extra features or even a shout-out by the creator.

4   Opportunity to shape the development of the channel

Another upside of having a community around you is that this community values the relationship they have with the creator over the videos they watch on a particular platform. A community will follow their favorite vlogger wherever they go.

It is incredibly challenging at any scale to make vlogs about nothing and replicate this time and time again. Being able to control a frame for 20 minutes by just talking alone with a camera to entertain millions of people is an art in itself. It also helps if the creator is relatable, like Emma Chamberlain.

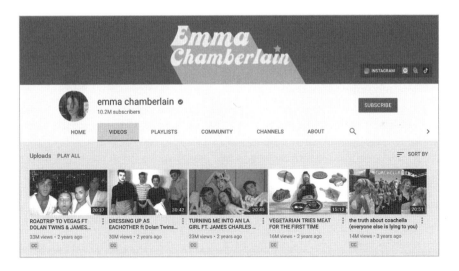

Emma Chamberlain's superpower is that she is super relatable.

Because her community of subscribers is based on a sense of belonging to a club of like-minded people, she can take her audience wherever she wants. Within four months, she's grown to 800,000 followers on TikTok.

5   Mutual benefits of participation

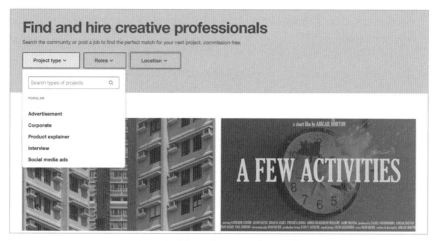

Vimeo's job board (vimeo.com/for-hire/)

Vimeo sees itself as a community for creative video and animation professionals. The platform adds value to its community members by functioning as a marketplace for professionals looking for creatives and creatives looking for a gig.

6   Precisely tailored content

Successful video producers don't just upload videos randomly. They know exactly what their audience wants. And if they're going to keep this audience interested and invested, they need to offer them more and better videos that are precisely tailored to them.

 See also Chapter 2.3 Find your content focus

If you are a successful community-based creator like Casey Neistat or Emma Chamberlain, you have the opportunity to build incredible depth with your audience. This depth can help you kick-start businesses and work with top-tier lifestyle brands who pay you to introduce your audience to them.

Why is it important?

"'Success' need not be complicated. Just start with making 1,000 people extremely, extremely happy." (Ferris, 2016)[98] This refers to Kevin Kelly's idea that thanks to the Internet, you no longer need a massive audience to make a living from your creative work; you just need the financial support of 1,000 truly passionate fans to create a sustainable livelihood through patronage. If 1,000 true fans each pay a video creator $12 per month, this creator earns $12,000 a month.

But 1,000 loyal customers are also a good enough basis for any business. See also: Seth Godin's Minimal Viable Audience.

The Conspiracy Collection Reveal | Jeffree Star x Shane Dawson

22,479,688 views · Oct 30, 2019   1.1M   20K   SHARE   SAVE   ...

On November 1, 2019, Shane Dawson and Jeffree Star launched a new cosmetics line called The Conspiracy Collection, which resulted in hours-long outages on Shopify and Morphe.com.

Understand how your audience uses video to drive community participation and connection, and let it inspire the ways you can authentically tell stories.

DriveTribe.com started with the three former Top Gear presenters, Jeremy Clarkson,
James May, and Richard Hammond.

For advertisers, partnering with creators who already have a large community gathered around them is a great way to borrow influence and increase relevance.

PREPARE - VIDEO STRATEGY AND PLANNING

It takes a lot of talent, focus, and perseverance to become successful.

You can be blessed with a couple of talents, and you can train yourself to become more persistent and not give up too soon.

But the focus part? That's strategy.

Strategy is all about focus: it will guide your decisions on what to do and what not to do. You don't want to waste time, energy, and money on video ideas that simply don't work. Nobody has time for that!

You're not here to get your 15 minutes of fame. You're in business because you want to play what inspirational speaker Simon Sinek calls "The Infinite Game." The basic premise of "The Infinite Game" is that there are at least two kinds of games: finite games and infinite games in life. Finite games aim to win. The purpose of the infinite game is to stay in the game for as long as possible in a sustainable way. (Sinek 2019)[99]

If you manage to get a million views on your YouTube or TikTok video, you win this time. But how will this pay your bills? How will this help you wake up every morning, eager to start the day? How can this one viral video help you stay in the game for as long as possible?

What you need is a video marketing strategy aligned with your goals for your business or you personally.

Strategy is just as much about what you're going to do as what you're not going to do. The framework I use for this is NOW-NEXT-NEW-NOT. It helps decide where to put the most effort. Choosing what to waste your money on is just as important as where your main focus (NOW) lies.

NOW: Focus the majority (70%) of your time, resources, and budget on what you know works for your target audience. If you have noticed that Facebook Video Ads are super-efficient, definitely don't stop doing them.

NEXT: Make room (20%) for improvement using video marketing to grow one particular segment of your target audience. Not reaching enough of your younger audience? Complement your current content strategy with topics that speak to a younger audience, like music or entertainment.

NEW: Want to be future proof? Assign 10% of your time, resources, and budget to experiments with content, tactics, and platforms you're not familiar with at all. The Return on Investment here is uncertain, but at least you're learning.

NOT: TikTok is not your thing? Nobody's judging you! Just make it clear that this is a no-go zone for you.

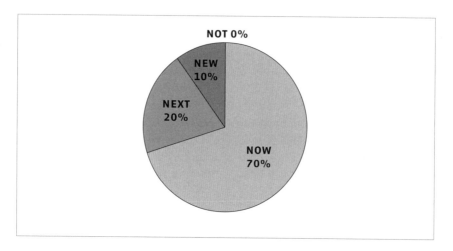

Assignment of time, resources, and budget

So what's the plan?

Please don't tell me it's "Going viral".

2.1 ARE YOU SURE YOU WANT TO "GO VIRAL"?

If you made it this far, chances are you've made up your mind: you're going to create and publish digital videos. And they're going to go viral and make you famous.

You have just fallen into a trap called magical thinking.

Magical thinking is the illusion that your ideas, thoughts, actions, words, or use of symbols can influence the course of events in the material world.

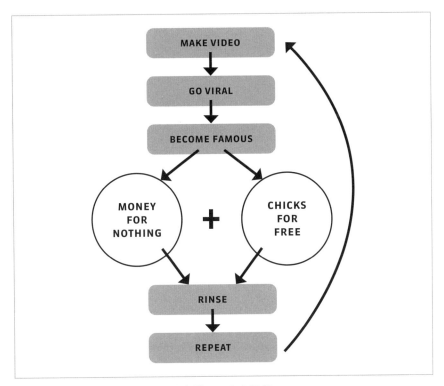

Viral video magical thinking

I'll make a video, and then it will go viral. I will become famous. Money for nothing and chicks for free. (Knopfler, 1985)[100]

I hate to break it to you, but this will probably not happen in your lifetime.

First of all: there is no such thing as an idea for a video, or video secrets you need to uncover, that will guarantee that you will make a video go viral. You can't make viral happen.

Rebecca Black - Friday

152,581,832 views • Sep 17, 2011   1.3M   3.9M   SHARE   SAVE   ...

In 2011, Rebecca's song "Friday" went viral for all the wrong reasons.

And secondly: are you sure you want to "go viral"?

2.1.1 **WHAT MAKES A VIDEO GO VIRAL?**

A viral video is a digital video that gets so much engagement from its viewers that it racks up millions of views.

Viral videos may be serious, and some are deeply emotional, but most are centered on entertainment and humorous content. (Wikipedia)[101]

There are all sorts of theories about what makes a video go viral. Depending on who you ask, viral video success is thought to be more likely if a video is humorous, shocking, dramatic, topical, warm, arousing, angry, scary, socially beneficial, cute, violent, sexy, uplifting, intriguing, quirky, interesting, authoritative, tear-jerking, educational, controversial or baby- and animal-filled. (Pirouz, Johnson, Thomson & Pirouz, 2015)[102]

Old Town Road
lil nas x
774.5K videos

Artist Lil Nas X promoted his song "Old Town Road" on TikTok with a meme showing people drinking "yee yee juice" that instantly transformed them into cowboys.

Does it help if videos are a bit... *weird*?

The majority of the videos in the YouTube Billion View Club are commercial music videos by famous artists.

"Despacito" (Luis Fonsi, 2017)

But the list also includes oddities, typically from TV programs aimed at children.

"Baby Shark Dance" (Pinkfong Kids' Songs & Stories, 2016)

By the way, some of the most popular YouTube channels are made exclusively for kids.

Kid-friendly animations channel "CoComelon – Nursery Rhymes" holds the record with 20-something videos in the YouTube Billion View Club.

2.1.2   POPULAR VIRAL VIDEO FORMATS

In his 2020 book *Attention Factory: The Story of TikTok and China's ByteDance*, Matthew Brennan distinguishes a handful of popular viral video types. He calls them video memes.

A meme is a concept or idea that spreads virally from one person to another via the Internet. An Internet meme could be anything from an image to an email or video file; however, the most common meme is an image of a person or animal with a funny or witty caption added to it. (Willaerts, 2018)[103]

Usually, they are humorous; they are copied and spread rapidly by Internet users, often with slight variations. It can be tough to find who initially started a meme. And sometimes old videos resurface, in a slightly altered form, to go viral.

Coffin Dance/Dancing Pallbearers. Originally a scene from a 2017 BBC item covering a group of Ghana pallbearers. In 2020, a popular TikTok video mashed this footage with a dance track called "Astronomia" by Russian artist Tony Igy.

1   Reveal memes involve a short setup, followed by a dramatic transformation or reveal following the structure of the accompanying song. The setup happens during the song's introduction, with the reveal beginning at the exact moment that the song's main riff or hook kicks in, amplifying the dramatic effect - a mini-story sequence compressed into 15 seconds.

DO THE HARLEM SHAKE (ORIGINAL)

54,416,963 views • Feb 2, 2013   👍 401K   👎 36K   ➔ SHARE   ≡+ SAVE   ...

"The Harlem Shake" (YouTube, 2013)

2   Dance memes involve mimicking a set sequence of novel dance moves or hand gestures that accompany the lyrics or beat. The portrait ratio of vertical video lends itself particularly well to capturing someone dancing.

Baby Ariel (musical.ly, 2016)

3   Challenge memes involve completing a difficult, unpleasant, or skillful task.

The "Ice bucket challenge" (2014) saw celebrities record themselves pouring buckets of ice water over their heads to raise awareness about Lou Gehrig's Disease.

(wikipedia.com)[104]

4   Filter memes are based on the use of a specific special effect. Although this was originally a Snapchat feature, TikTok quickly realized that users would adopt innovative and fun AR video filters to create memes.

An example is the 2020 "Mirror reflection challenge" on TikTok. The filter used here simply mirrored the left half of the screen onto the right side.

RISKS INVOLVING VIRAL VIDEOS

1   Attention has a very short life cycle! Viewer engagement is usually temporary, visceral, and noisy.

2   If it's controversial, it's usually not advertiser-friendly, so no ad revenue or sponsorships.

3   Your newfound audience will start watching your stupid old videos.

4   Context collapse: videos uploaded by regular people usually have no or very poor metadata. It's typically unclear who created the material and why.

5   Cancel culture: sometimes, a video goes viral for all the wrong reasons. People are super touchy about politics, minorities, or religion. The more successful you are, the higher the chance that you will run into trouble.

Cancel culture is a form of boycott after a (famous) person has made a controversial statement or action in the present or the past. Large groups go online to "out" this person and pressure any employers to stop working with them. This phenomenon became popular around 2017.

Shane Dawson ✔
@shanedawson   ...

I deleted everything. I'm done. For those who wanted me to "address it" I did. I'm sure u can find it reposted somewhere. But I don't want this energy in my life or on my timeline. I'm too sensitive for this shit and I'm done.

09:23 · 21/06/2020 · Twitter for iPhone

4.959 Retweets **9.796** Quote Tweets **186K** Likes

YouTuber Shane Dawson got canceled in 2020 after old videos of him in blackface resurfaced.

While viral success on a platform doesn't necessarily translate into more sales or customers, it can be a nice bonus in some cases. Based on viral videos on TikTok's For You page, the conversion rate from viewers to followers is around 0.3% to 1%. That means a video with one million views will potentially lead to 3,000 to 10,000 new followers. (Günel 2020)[105]

2.2 IDENTIFY YOUR BIGGEST CHALLENGES

There's no point in spending time and money creating nice videos if you don't know what you want to achieve with them or what your ultimate goal is. (Trip, 2020)[106]

To define your video marketing strategy, you need to start with the end in mind. What is the difference that you want your videos to make? Which of your business, marketing, or personal problems are these videos going to help you solve?

1   Brand awareness: your target audience isn't aware of your brand.

2   Prospects choose the competition instead of you. You lose them in the "messy middle" between considering your brand and converting.

3   You're trying to make money with your videos but to no avail. Sales leads don't convert to customers.

4   Customers stop using your service. Can video marketing prevent or fix this?

You have fans, but none of them create videos to recommend you to their peers spontaneously.

2.2.1 THE TARGET AUDIENCE ISN'T AWARE OF YOUR BRAND

Your potential customers have a problem, and you have a solution - you just haven't found each other yet. Why is this? Why aren't target audiences aware of your business (yet)? And how can you fix this?

If you want to change the fact that nobody knows you, you need to work on your Brand Awareness.

Jeff Bezos once defined a brand as the following: "Your brand is what people say about you when you're not in the room." A brand can be represented by your business name, your product name, or even your name or nickname.

Being a brand that comes to mind both quickly and fluently to customers is what matters, and a massive T.V. spend alone is no longer the best way to achieve this. (Mowat, 2018)[107]

American speaker Tony Robbins, one of the most famous personal branding examples, uses video marketing to find customers for his seminars.

If you're doing it right, your brand is always represented in a consistent, recognizable way. Online, this can be the username or handle that you use to represent your business, product/service, or even you as an individual. This includes the name and visual elements like your logo, profile picture, visual style, etc.

Nothing builds a brand like emotion, and nothing drives emotion like video. (Howe, 2021)[108]

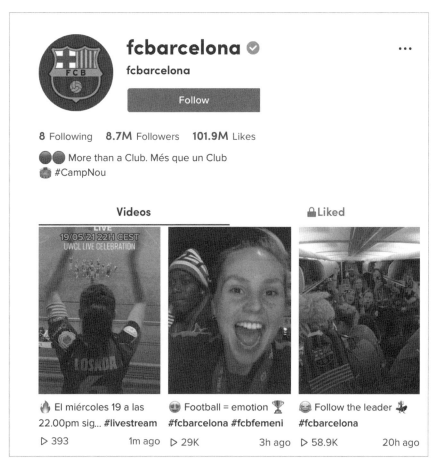

On TikTok, football team FC Barcelona was the most followed sports account of 2020.

Like Coca-Cola, some of the world's most famous brands have it easier to translate their brand strategy in how they use video as a content strategy.

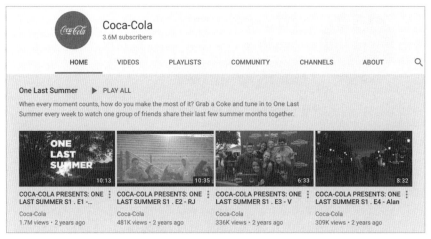

Coca-Cola's YouTube channel boasts millions of subscribers from all over the world.

Video is a trendy format with brands of all sorts. Brand awareness videos are typically entertaining, using a soft-sell approach to ingrain the brand's name and image into viewers' minds. (Miller, 2018)[109]

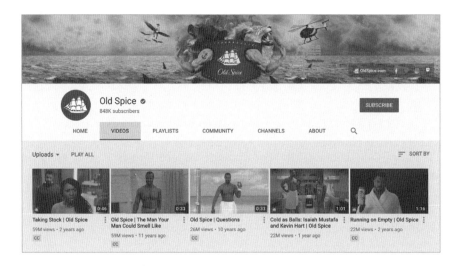

An excellent example of how videos can create brand awareness is the series of videos produced by Old Spice.

But what if you've just started? How can video marketing help you become a more well-known brand?

How do you stand out in a sea of videos?

Hypothesis 1: Create videos that make them stop scrolling

In online environments like YouTube, Facebook, or TikTok, your videos have to compete for attention with literally millions of others. How do you make your audience stop scrolling through their feed and click on your video?

Just like with fishing, you reel them in with a hook. A hook point creates a curiosity gap in your viewer's mind. In "Hook Point: How to Stand Out in a 3-Second World," out of the box thinker Brendan Kane states that: "These days, if you want to get your message out to the world, you often have as little as three seconds to do so [...] If you can't capture people's attention in that first three seconds, or whatever short time period you have with them, then you can't get them to pay attention to the rest of your story, products, or services." (Kane, 2020)[110]

A Hook Point can be comprised of:

- text (e.g., a phrase, title, or piece of copy),
- an insight (from statistics or a professional's point of view, a philosophy, or a person's thought),
- a concept/idea or a format (e.g., an image or video),
- a personality or performance (e.g., music, sports, acting, or a cadence),
- a product/service, or
- a combination of some or all of these elements.

If your video title needs a hook to convince them to click, the thumbnail is often what sells it. If you can make your audience look at the thumbnail and wonder, "What's going on here?" you've successfully created a curiosity gap. You have their attention.

They've clicked on your video! So how do you make sure they don't quit after a few seconds?

 Don't waste your viewers' time or bandwidth! Deliver your value at a quick and satisfying pace rather than a slow and methodical one. (Kane, 2020)[111]

Traditional story arcs manipulate the audience's attention by building up tension towards one major, revealing climax.

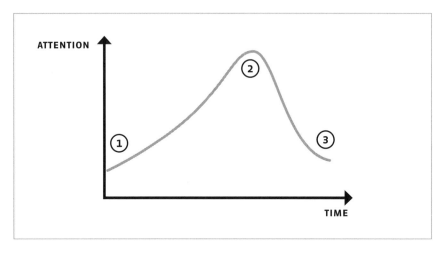

Manipulation of the audience's attention vs. time in a traditional story arc

Successful online videos use multiple peaks and unexpected shifts in what is called a heartbeat narrative structure. (Think With Google)[112]

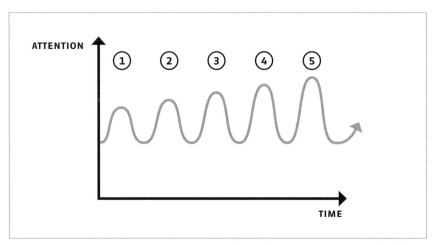

Heartbeat narrative structure of successful online videos

Here's what that could look like:

1   GREETING. *"Hi, it's Clo..."* You have no idea in what context people will watch your video, so get your branding out there right away.

2   HOOK. Make people want to stay to see what's going to happen. *"In this short video, I'm going to show/teach/explain how/why/what/who/where you can [solve a problem]..."* Get right to the point. Assure them this video is exactly what they expected it to be after clicking.

3   RELATE. *"Has it happened to you ...?"* Make the connection with your audience's context.

4   HEARTBEATS. Multiple peaks and unexpected shifts are what keeps the central part of the story going. Don't waste your viewers' time, e.g., by rambling or going on a tangent.

5   WRAP-UP and CALL TO ACTION. Thank your audience for their time and tell them where to go next:

   • Subscribe to your channel, turn on notifications, follow your video account
   • Comment, like, share your video
   • Download chart/templates/spreadsheet/cheat sheet
   • Get this deal/goodies/freebies
   • Register for event
   • Schedule a call with you
   • Join your mailing list
   • Follow you on social media

Hypothesis 2: Create videos with high production value

Production value is the quality of the video production. For premium brands like Mercedes or Nike, nothing less than professionally made videos are expected. Their audience wouldn't accept videos with blurry images, lousy audio, or bad editing. If anything annoys viewers, preventing them from watching it until the end, this will show in your retention data.

High expectations are held when people are watching premium streaming services like Netflix. Nobody wants to pay $15 a month to watch images that are so shaky they make you seasick.

Videos with high production value do have their place on YouTube, TikTok, Facebook, or LinkedIn – especially if they're music videos, movie trailers, or video ads. Announcement videos, trailers, and promo videos are a great way to announce new team members, press releases, or exciting things in your company's pipeline, for example.

But production value doesn't dictate success on social platforms; success comes from telling authentic and compelling stories. (Kane, 2020)[113] YouTube, Facebook, and TikTok audiences prefer the authenticity of raw, scrappy production quality; don't alienate them with high production value and overdone gloss. YouTube, in particular, has a do-it-yourself ethic; it is punk T.V. for the 21st century. (Stokel-Walker, 2018)[114]

One of the most common mistakes beginners make is to sink their entire budget into one high-quality video and hope that they get the success they are hoping for from that video. (Samuel, 2020)[115]

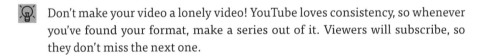 Don't make your video a lonely video! YouTube loves consistency, so whenever you've found your format, make a series out of it. Viewers will subscribe, so they don't miss the next one.

For longer videos, such as podcasts or interviews, improve the viewer experience by cutting a longer video up into shorter pieces, or by using the Chapters feature (on YouTube).

The balance between quantity and quality depends on the audience's expectations of that particular platform. On TikTok, your frequency can be very high, and production quality can be somewhat lower. On LinkedIn, your production quality should be very high, but your frequency can be lower.

Want to see results faster? Use video ads.

Hypothesis 3: Use video advertising

Video ads are not just ads that promote your video or your channel. They have become a powerful weapon in digital marketing professionals' arsenal. Compared to other advertising formats, video ads merge two things that catch user attention: movement and sound.

Promotional videos (for a product, an initiative, or a service) are perfect for more extensive content campaigns.

Not every video ad has to be a video in the strict sense of the word. Slideshows or carousels are also popular formats for video ads.

 Use one of the many affordable do-it-yourself video ad platforms like Animoto, Magisto, Promo.com or Lumen5. With these online tools, you can create new video ads using the image and video assets you already have – or make use of stock images and videos.

Overview of video platforms and their video advertising capabilities

	VIMEO	YOUTUBE	WISTIA	TWITCH	INSTAGRAM	SNAPCHAT	TWITTER	TIKTOK	FACEBOOK	LINKEDIN	PINTEREST
Video ads?	No	Yes	No	Yes	Yes	No	Yes	Yes	Yes	Yes	Yes

YouTube video ads

With YouTube ads, reach potential customers and have them take action when they watch or search for videos on YouTube – and only pay when they show interest. You can create an ad that appears before a video starts or alongside a video on its watch page on YouTube. The available YouTube formats are Skippable video ads, Non-skippable video ads, and Bumper ads.

YouTube Ads are engaging because you can target people who are both actively interested and already engaging in content relevant to your ad.

All you have to do is create your ad, set your budget, and target the desired audience. There's no minimum price to run an ad - and you can change your ads, targeting, and budgets at any time. You can also end your campaign whenever you want. (YouTube Creator Academy)[116]

Targeting is key! If you're targeting too broadly, you will have a meager return on investment of your campaign. Plus, you potentially annoy lots of people.

 Don't target demographic: this is rarely an indicator of buying intent or interest in a particular topic.

➕ **Want to know more?**

- Best practices for video campaigns[117]: helpful guides from the YouTube team.
- YouTube Re:View Newsletter[118] with Trends, Creators, Insights. Get the latest inspiration from YouTube sent to your inbox.
- YouTube Ads Leaderboard[119] showcases the top ads that people choose to watch each month.
- YouTube success stories[120]: See how businesses of all sizes are reaching their goals with YouTube Ads.
- Google Ads Video Certification (Skillshop, 2019)[121]
- YouTube success stories[122]: See how businesses of all sizes are reaching their goals with YouTube Ads.
- YouTube Advertising News and Inspiration[123]: the latest product releases, trending video ads, success stories, and more.
- YouTube Works Awards[124]: an annual, global celebration of the best campaigns across YouTube captivates not only audiences but also generates results.

TikTok video ads

TikTok, the leading destination for short-form mobile video, provides various full-screen vertical short-form video content. Video ads on TikTok are called BuzzVideo, TopBuzz, and Babe; they can be in-feed ads, details page ads, or story ads.

 When developing creative for your campaign, keep in mind that TikTok evolves fast and is changing every day. Keep experimenting with new creative formats.

Want to know more?

- TikTok For Business Creative Center (TikTok for Business)[125]
- TikTok Blog: Updates, insights, and creative inspiration from our vibrant business community on TikTok (TikTok for Business)[126]
- TikTok For Business Small Business Resource Center (TikTok for Business)[127]
- 9 creative tips to drive performance (TikTok for Business Creative Center)[128]
- TikTok for Business Europe tiktokforbusinesseurope.com
- TikTok Creator Marketplace: The official platform for brand and creator collaborations on TikTok creatormarketplace.tiktok.com

Video ads on Instagram

Instagram recommends including movement and sound to capture attention quickly, show unique features of a product, or tell your brand story. There are three main types of video ads on Instagram: video ads in the Instagram feed, Stories as video ads, or Video ads in IGTV.

The Instagram Feed displays photos and videos from accounts that people follow and from advertisers. You can use the video format in Instagram Feed to show off your product, service, or brand in new ways.

Want to know more?

- Facebook Video Ad Specs for Instagram Feed Video Views (Facebook for Business)[129]
- Use filters, stickers, and text to create engaging ads with the Instagram Stories camera. (Facebook For Business)[130]
- Facebook IQ articles about video ads on Instagram[131]

Twitch video ads

Twitch video ads are "high-impact display units and unskippable ads that weave directly into live broadcasts." Like most livestreaming services, Twitch offers advertising options for brands looking to promote their products and services. Their main video advertising format is called Twitch Premium Video. (Twitch Advertising)[132]

Not only does Twitch support traditional ad placements like pre-roll videos and banners, but advertisers can also find and partner with Twitch influencers. (Influencer Marketing Hub, 2021)[133]

Want to know more?

- Twitch Advertising switch advertising.tv

Facebook video ads

Facebook is undeniably the most popular video-sharing platform after YouTube. Video ads on Facebook can be displayed In-stream, in the Facebook Feed, or Facebook Stories.

Want to know more?

- Facebook Video Ad Formats (Facebook for Business)[134]
- Facebook Blueprint tutorials[135]
- The essential guide to finding visuals for your ads (Facebook Blueprint Course)[136]
- Facebook Business Help Center about Video Ads[137]

Twitter video ads

Video ads on Twitter can be Standalone Video Ads, Video Ads with Conversation Buttons, or Video Ads with Polls.

Want to know more?

- Twitter for Business business.twitter.com

LinkedIn video ads

Video ads on LinkedIn are a Sponsored Content ad format that appears in the LinkedIn feed. Video is frequently used in ads and the recently launched LinkedIn Stories format.

➕ Want to know more?

- The Fundamental Strategies for Video Ads on LinkedIn: A Guide to High-Performing Creative (LinkedIn Marketing Solutions)[138]
- LinkedIn Video Ads Best Practices (LinkedIn Marketing Solutions)[139]
- The Fundamental Strategies of Video Ads on LinkedIn (LinkedIn Marketing Solutions)[140]

Pinterest video ads

Pinterest video ads are integrated into the feed to appear alongside organic pins.

➕ Want to know more?

- Pinterest Business business.pinterest.com
- Pinterest Business creator newsletter: Be the first to hear about product launches, emerging trends, and inspiring content ideas. (Pinterest Business)[141]

Hypothesis 4: Make your visual identity pop

Video platforms may adapt and change, but it doesn't take away from the fact that standing out is critical as they become inundated with content. (Kane, 2020)[142]

The identity of your channel or account, for example, your profile picture or channel art, helps to:

- encapsulate your brand
- be recognizable to your audience
- be easy to remember

Think of your visual identity as a mirror: what does it reveal about you? Your name, profile picture or logo, overall design: what does every element tell you about yourself or your brand?

Every video platform allows for different degrees of customization of your primary identity, like your Channel or Account. A channel name is similar to a social media handle. Select a channel name that you like and that represents you:

- business name (if you already have a business, use that)
- own name
- creative name, for example, for your project

 Don't overthink your channel name – it's usually changeable (although you might lose your Verified Account status).

It's a good idea to make your branding:

- Clear and representative so that people who find you will instantly understand what your videos are all about.
- As simple as possible. Think of logos or branding of products you like - they're likely a singular image that sticks in your brain.
- Something you're proud of. Remember - your channel branding will become an extension of you, especially if you star in your channel. (YouTube Creator Academy)[143]

Your Channel Art or profile header is a larger banner space for you to show what you're all about. TikTok and Instagram don't offer profile headers, though the latter does allow you to add "highlights" instead. Many creators include their upload schedule and their primary calls-to-action here, like the URL of their main website.

 You can create your channel art in your favorite photo editing software. Canva is a popular resource for making banners.

Your Channel Description or bio gives viewers an overview of what they can expect from you. It could describe the types of content you will produce, include your upload schedule, and note who is starring in your videos. You can also include links to your website, contact info, or links to your other social media accounts.

 On Instagram and TikTok, you can only add one link. "Link in bio" type services are an excellent option if you only have one slot. These platforms allow you to integrate all of your websites and social media links in one place. Examples: Koji, Sked, Mona, Milkshake, Linktree, Flooz, Beacons, and Snipfeed.

The Channel Trailer (called "Featured Content" on YouTube) is the video equivalent of the "About Us" section on websites. It's not an option on TikTok but works well on Twitch and YouTube. On Instagram, you can use highlights instead.

 Not sure what to talk about in your channel trailer? Make it about your name.

If your channel identity centers around a brand name, explain where this name came from.

- Is it an acronym? If yes, what does it stand for? What does this say about the origins of the organization?
- Is it named after a person? If yes, what was their role? Where are they now?

If your channel identity is your name or nickname:

- How did you get your name?
- What's your full name? Do you like it?
- Do you know the meaning of your name and why your parents chose it? Do you think it suits you? What about your children's names?

- If you could choose any other name for yourself, what would it be?
- If you were named based on your traits, habits, or likes, what would your name be?

If you're hesitant to put yourself out there, there are business benefits to using video marketing to promote your personal brand.

Here's what Gary Vaynerchuck says about personal branding: "It's important to build a personal brand because it's the only thing you're going to have. Your reputation online and in the new business world is pretty much the game, so you've got to be a good person. You can't hide anything, and more importantly, you've got to be out there at some level."

The best content creators inform, inspire, educate, entertain, and build community all at once. (Cannel & Travis, 2018)[144]

Your personal brand can be a starting point for other businesses. Please stick to your niche and teach others how you did it with educational videos. Use YouTube, TikTok, Instagram, or Facebook to test video engagement and consult video analytics.

Video marketing is a perfect fit for people who are an expert at something and who want to create a business offering:

- Consulting services
- Speaking gigs
- Online courses

For many video creators, their face is their logo. If you want to stand out in a sea of video faces, a good profile picture is not enough. You need to create a consistent and recognizable personal style.

What you wear, your speaking style, graphics, sound effects, and even the background in your videos are all part of your personal style. You don't have to be a celebrity or influencer to gain substantial traffic, nor do you have to create highly produced corporate videos; you just have to be you.

It's more interesting for the audience if you're the opposite of normal. So be an extreme character. The spotlight is the excuse. You can get away with anything in the name of entertainment. It can be a version of yourself, or it can be a mask. (It's easier to be honest behind a mask.) (Sivers, 2020)[145]

The fact that you think you're "too awkward" in your video or that your video is "too unprofessional" may be your secret superpower.

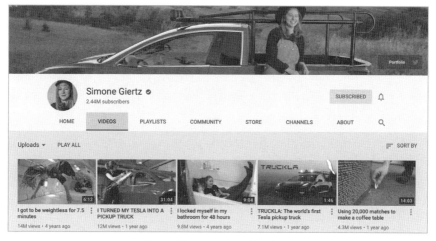

Simone Giertz creates terrible robots.

Ignore the little voice inside your head that says, "They're all gonna laugh at me." We all cringe when we see our old videos.

SAN DIEGO
Me at the zoo
66,392,398 views • Apr 24, 2005   7.8M   186K   SHARE   SAVE   ...

"Me at the zoo", the first uploaded video available to YouTube, features a cringe-worthy monologue by YouTube founder Jawed Karim.

 As your audience grows, so will the chance of criticism. Whatever happens: strive to be "unflappable yet nice" to your audience and your competitors.

The unflappable part will help you cope with criticism. Strive to be:

- Confident in the public eye, even in the face of criticism. My advice: never let them see you bleed. Never complain, never explain. Show your human side but never get personal.
- A consistent hard worker who is known to produce high-quality videos every time.

- Open-minded, even about your expertise. Listen to your community and act on their suggestions for improvement.
- Friendly and pleasant to work with.

You don't have to be the very best. Leading your audience with your expertise, your confidence, your integrity, and your passion is enough.

2.2.2 PROSPECTS CHOOSE THE COMPETITION INSTEAD OF YOU

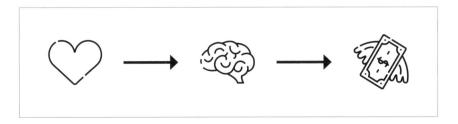

How people buy: from the heart to the brain, to the wallet

How do your customers choose you? By realizing that the buying decision process is not always a simple, linear process. Although consumers may have decided in their hearts what to buy, they will carry out a research phase to arm themselves against future disappointment. Internet personality Gary Vaynerchuk calls this process "from the heart to brain to wallet."

In marketing circles, this corresponds to the first three phases in the Customer Journey - the imaginary journey a consumer makes when they're going through their buying decision process.

Heart, brain wallet mapped to Customer Journey framework

CUSTOMER JOURNEY	SEE (Awareness)	THINK (Considera-tion)	BUY (Activation)	USE (Loyalty)	LOVE (Advocacy)
	Problem ➜ Solution	Solution ➜ Product/ Service	Product/ Service ➜ Sale	Sale ➜ Satisfaction	Satisfaction ➜ Referral
	♡	🧠	💵		

Heart, Brain, Wallet mapped to the Sales process

CONVERSION GOAL	♡	🧠	💵		
	suspect → potential lead → lead	lead → potential buyer	potential buyer → buyer	buyer → repeat buyer	repeat buyer → fan

Sales professionals flip this journey model to create a sales funnel that aligns with the customer's imaginary journey.

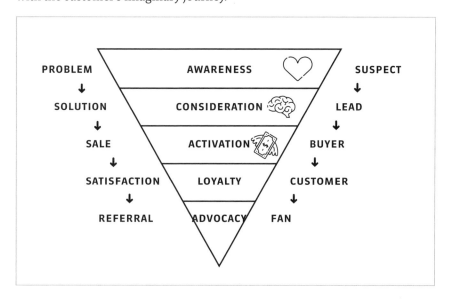

Heart, brain, wallet vs. Sales funnel

So why is the sales journey more like a funnel than a pipeline? Why do you lose some of your potential customers along the way?

There's a lot more going on between awareness and activation:

- Prospects Google for product information and maybe even price comparison
- Prospects are open to customer reviews of the same product.

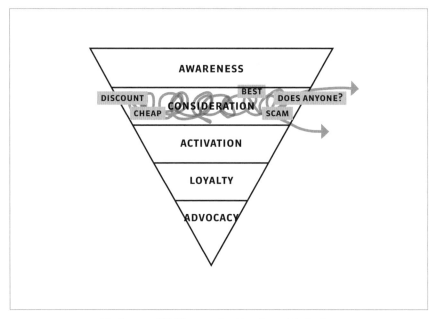

The "messy middle" between Consideration and Activation

Google calls this "the messy middle" of the purchase journey. When it comes to making everyday decisions, we're a lot less rational than we think. Logical reasoning often gives way to our emotions, so we end up making decisions that surprise even ourselves. (Google, 2020)[146]

When (subconsciously) entering the consideration phase in their customer journey, people look for signals that confirm the buying decision they've already made in their hearts. They might even look for approval from their peers by asking their friends and family what their experience with this product or service was. Very often, this takes the form of an open question or a quick Story on social media platforms like Facebook or Instagram:

- "Who has experience with [product/service]? Would you recommend?"
- "Looking for a [product category]. Is [product name] any good?"

Depending on the buyer and the product category, people also use Google Search to look for alternatives:

- Same product, but at a lower price, e.g., by combining product name with search terms like discount codes, promo, cheap,...

- Same solution, but other product/service, e.g., by combining category name with "best."

This process can be time-consuming. The purchase decision can unexpectedly become more complex than initially expected – especially for products that:

- involve high-budget, e.g., cars or real estate
- require you to change your daily routines, e.g., sports equipment
- have a potential impact on how your peers will perceive you, e.g., tattoos

So buyers might postpone the buying decision and come back later for a second, and then a third look, and so on.

The Google study "Decoding Decisions - Making sense of the messy middle" (Google, 2020)[147], names six cognitive biases that may influence people's eventual buying decision:

- **Power of now**: The longer you have to wait for a product, the weaker the proposition becomes.
- **Social proof**: Recommendations and reviews from others can be very persuasive.
- **Scarcity bias**: As stock or availability of a product decreases, the more desirable it becomes.
- **Authority bias**: Being swayed by an expert or trusted source.
- **Power of free**: A free gift with a purchase, even if unrelated, can be a powerful motivator. Give give give, and sometimes you will receive. (Sivers, 2020)[148]
- **Category heuristics**: key product specs that simplify decisions.

How can video marketing help these potential customers out of the messy middle and straight back to you?

Hypothesis 1: Convince with a sales video

With a sales video, you're interrupting someone's day. Nobody wakes up thinking: "I'm ready to get sold to." The fact that an entire video is a call-to-action (to buy the product) makes it a sales video. Compelling sales videos have a Heartbeat Narrative Structure. An example:

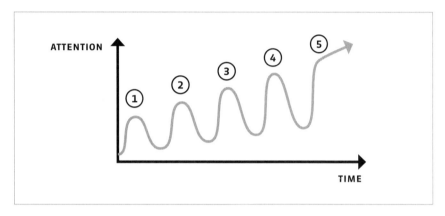

Outline for a short and snappy promotional video

1 CONNECT: Relate to your audience's obstacles, problems, and challenges when trying to reach their goals: *"You know how ..." "Do you want X? But feel like Y?" "Do you dream of X? But find that Y?"*

2 SOLUTION: Share the Value Proposition (= how your product solves their problems) *"Well, what we do is ..."* Tell them about, *"This one system to follow,"* or, *"This set of steps to follow,"* or, *"If you had this mindset, you'd have success as I have."*

3 USP: Answer to "Why should I buy it from YOU" (= your Unique Selling Proposition or USP) Answer the unspoken question, "Why us?" - or you risk losing the sale to a better-defined competitor.

4 SOCIAL PROOF: Offer proof of your expertise by quoting happy customers. Answer to "Why should I trust you?" *"You don't have to take my word for it. In fact, ..."*

5   CALL TO ACTION: The introduction of the ideal action you want your viewers to take. Online: follow, subscribe, register, download, buy, order. Offline:
call, visit.

 Don't let your sales video end abruptly. Give your viewers some breathing
space to follow up on the call to action.

Hypothesis 2: With video formats that counter the buyer's bias

1   Product demo video or product highlighter video

A product demo or product highlighter video:

- Explains the benefits of using the product
- Is functional, clean, and simple
- Highlights only the product and its features, benefits, and uses
- Is usually a video with the product on a plain, white background.

 Front-load your USP and keep it short.

*Vat19.com's YouTube channel consists of funny product demos, each of them raking in
hundreds of thousands of views.*

 If you can: show, don't tell. Show the product in the context of people
using it.

Product video: Hiking and camping equipment by Decathlon on Quechua.com.[149]

The most efficient context of a product video is on the product page of an e-commerce store. Take, for example, Amazon product videos. The following picks from Amazon Product Video Guidelines (Amazon Seller Central, 2021) can be used as best practices for sales video overall:

- Any claims you make (implied or explicit) must be supported by evidence. You may provide your personal opinion, provided it is noted as such.
- Any claim that could reasonably be interpreted as a factual statement must be accurate and substantiated.
- Any products used must be yours, and you must be the brand owner.
- Videos must not contain prices, promotion information, discount claims (including words such as "cheap," "affordable," "on sale," etc.), or time-sensitive information.
- If you mention customer reviews, you must include accurate product information that can be substantiated. Any customer review details must be less than one year old.

Things to avoid in a sales video (and every video, for that matter):

- Health claims, medical claims, or medical advice.
- Financial claims or financial advice.
- Controversial, political, sensitive, or sexually suggestive content.
- Defamatory or derogatory statements about competitor products or brands. (Statements about competing products are ok, but they must be factual.)

And what about *service* videos? E.g., videos where you show that you go the extra mile during lockdown periods by accepting orders via the web. Or that show how your personnel abides by the general rules and regulations due to the pandemic.

Sometimes all a customer needs is a little nudge to try your products and services. A video on your Google My Business profile provides precisely that. (Wave.video, 2021)[150]

 Uploading short videos to your Google My Business profile is a quick win. The maximum file size is only 75 MB per video, though!

Google My Business (GMB) is a free Internet-based service designed by Google to help promote local businesses online. It's a tool that enables business owners to manage how they appear online across Google Search and make their business stand out.

 Videos also give people a reason to pay more attention to new products. You can take advantage of the strength of video content by cross-posting the same videos on your social media channels such as YouTube, Facebook, or Instagram! (GMBGorilla, 2020)[151]

2   Explainer video

Explainer videos are short marketing videos that explain a product or company. They show people how to solve a problem or learn a new trick and are usually embedded on a website or landing page.

Our Blades Are F***ing Great" by DollarShaveClub.com is an epic example of an explainer video.

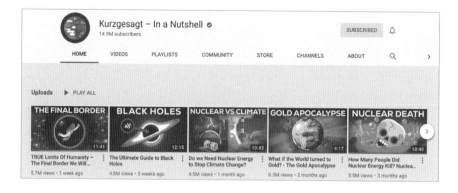

German animation studio Kurzgesagt's YouTube channel focuses on minimalist animated educational content, discussing scientific, technological, political, philosophical, and psychological subjects.

They can feature someone explaining the benefits of the product or use animation with a voice-over.

Animation is usually generated digitally by starting from some type of artwork and can be 2-dimensional or 3-dimensional. 2D animation often implies creating characters, objects, and backgrounds. The illusion of movement is created when individual drawings are sequenced together over time. 3D animation combines 3D models of objects and programmed or hand "keyframed" movements. Things modeled in a 3D environment can spin and turn around, which is impossible in 2D animation.

Whiteboard movies are recorded in front of a whiteboard (Moz style) or animated video that looks like it is being drawn on a whiteboard. Whiteboard animation involves an author (usually only visualized as a hand holding a marker pen) who physically draws and records an illustrated story using a whiteboard, or whiteboard-like surface. Whiteboard movies are gaining in popularity because they are less expensive to make than regular animation videos.

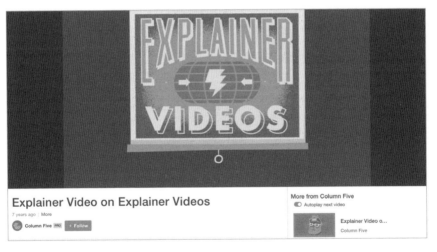

Explainer Video on Explainer Videos by Column Five on Vimeo.

 By creating a how-to video about your product, you are leveraging the fact that many people go to YouTube to simply learn new things.

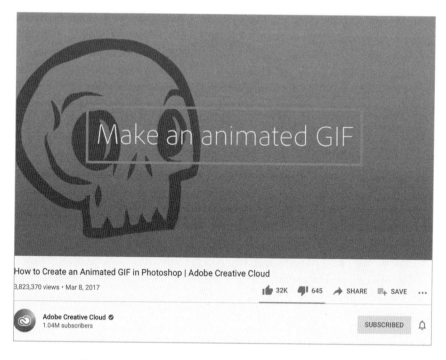

How to Create an Animated GIF in Photoshop by Adobe Creative Cloud.

3   Customer experience video or customer review video

A customer experience video is usually captured by the reviewers, fans, or customers. It offers a realistic experience so that other buyers understand the product better.

OnePlus 6 Review: Right On the Money!
21,711,161 views • May 25, 2018   109K   3.9K   SHARE   SAVE   ...

Marques "MKBHD" Brownlee reviews the OnePlus 6 smartphone in 2018.

Find someone who is an expert in reviewing products and convince them to try your product. You can also find more technically inclined users and encourage them to create videos about what they like about your product. For instance, this can be a detailed walk-through of a specific feature or an overall look at how you can use the product.

The shopping haul – a YouTuber buying a lot of products and trying them out at home (in front of a camera) – is a staple of the lifestyle element of YouTube. (Stokel-Walker, 2018)[152] A haul video is a video recording posted to the Internet. A person discusses items that they recently purchased, sometimes going into detail about their experiences during the purchase and the cost of the things they bought. (Wikipedia)[153]

An unboxing video is a recording of yourself opening items for the first time. Unboxing videos are wildly popular on YouTube. Unboxing videos initially focused on fashion or high-tech products. Today, the competition to unbox top tech gadgets - such as the latest iPhones or gaming consoles - is fierce. (ExpertVoice)[154]

Unboxing The $20,000 Smartphone

19,188,797 views • Dec 25, 2016

👍 264K   👎 17K   ➤ SHARE   ⊟₊ SAVE   ...

Unbox Therapy ✔
17.9M subscribers

JOIN   SUBSCRIBE

Unbox Therapy, "where products get naked".

4   Testimonials and case studies

Testimonials and case study videos act as social proof reinforcing the claims made by the brand, adding a layer of reassurance.

Customer testimonials feature real people who have used your product and talk about the difference it made to their life. You can even create a montage of your best customer testimonials.

Case study videos demonstrate how a product or service helps its customers. Case studies are based on statistics and customers' specific success with your product or service. They make your clients look like thought leaders and show off your product or service in a great light. The more factual and data-based you can make your case study videos, the greater their effect.

Salesforce customer testimonial by Burberry's Angela Ahrendts.

   Do not recruit actors for your testimonial videos! Contact your satisfied client base instead, and ask them to come up with an honest video testimonial. (Olson, 2020)[155]

   Organizing or sponsoring a business event? Ask your customer service team to suggest customers who want to speak with you and ask for their permission to record a testimonial video with them.

5   Video retargeting

Video remarketing or retargeting is a cost-effective way to show (video) ads to people who have already interacted with your website and your videos.

The first time your audience interacts with you, the resulting user data permits Google or Facebook to create a remarketing list. A remarketing list is a collection of website visitors or app users gathered by snippets of code hidden in a website or an app. This list is then used to show these visitors the second round of ads.

How does it work for video? You can retarget with a video ad, or retarget from video, or a combination of both.

Let's have a look at that last category. On YouTube, this works as follows :

YouTube creates a remarketing list of people who have seen your YouTube videos or have interacted with your YouTube channel:

- Viewed any video from a channel
- Viewed certain videos
- Viewed any video (as an ad) from a channel
- Viewed specific videos (as ads)
- Subscribed to a channel
- Visited a channel home page
- Liked any video from a channel
- Added any video from a channel to a playlist
- Shared any video from a channel

You can then use this remarketing list to show personalized ads to people on YouTube, Search, Shopping, and Gmail.

Want to use video remarketing to convince potential customers who are stuck in the messy middle?

1   Create a lure video that is irresistible to your target audience. A lure video exposes your target audience to a real problem they may be facing, e.g., "Top 10 mistakes...". A lure video has high production value but does not ask for any commitment from the viewer.

2   Upload this video natively to your platform of choice, e.g., Facebook Page or YouTube channel. Boost with advertising if you want to go faster.

3   Use Facebook or Google/YouTube ads for retargeting anyone who has watched the majority of your video.

4   The remarketing video is short but has a heavy focus on sales conversion.

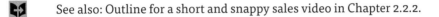 See also: Outline for a short and snappy sales video in Chapter 2.2.2.

6   Videos in email marketing

Like peanut butter and jelly, video and email are better together. (Wistia, 2019)[156]

Video:

- Boosts email click-through rates,
- Adds an enticing interactive component to communication, and
- Makes email feel like less of a chore for your audience.

The most well-known video email marketing platforms are BombBomb and Wistia. BombBomb's software lets you record and send videos directly to anyone from your computer or smartphone (iOS and Android). Wistia is a solid video hosting platform, focusing on video analytics that you can actually use.

Can you embed a video in an email?

If you're sporting some technical know-how and feel comfortable with HTML, then you may consider embedding video in your emails. Be aware, however, that most email clients do not support playing video in the inbox. Notable exceptions (EmailOnAcid, 2018)[157]:

- Apple Mail
- Outlook for Mac
- iOS 10+ (mail app)
- Samsung Galaxy (mail app)

Other clients like Gmail and Android devices will display a fallback image. (CampaignMonitor, 2021)[158]

 Use Ezgif.com to create a GIF from your video and add that to your email message. Add a play button overlay to your GIF to encourage subscribers to click through to your video.

2.2.3 ## SALES LEADS DON'T CONVERT TO CUSTOMERS

You want your videos to convert. Conversion is any action that follows from the video but isn't about the video (or the video channel) itself. So not just watching or engaging, but clicking buttons, visiting websites, downloading white papers, or buying products.

How can video marketing help?

Hypothesis 1: Lead your viewers to a landing page

Most video platforms offer viewer, follower, or subscriber analytics. But none of these data allows you to take the conversation off the platform.

How do you sell with a video?

Step 1: Get their permission to continue the conversation via email

To put it bluntly: you need to capture their contact data and add it to your CRM or marketing automation tool.

How? By making them a free but irresistible offer, for example, the Ultimate Guide or some other valuable content asset in pdf form. To download the pdf, your prospects need to fill in their contact data and opt-in to receive updates about your product or service via email.

Step 2: Get their financial data

Make a foot-in-the-door offer: a low-priced service or product (I've been told the sweet spot is around $7). Sales is a numbers game: there's a 50-60% chance they'll buy more later. But they are now in your system, and if your platform of choice allows for it, you can automate upselling offers by email.

Step 3: Upsell, cross-sell, and stimulate customer loyalty

This is where scaling becomes interesting:

- Make your potential buyers a gateway offer. Example: pay only shipping costs to get a free copy of your book.
- Make your actual buyers the main offer.
- Sell your repeat buyers your profit booster.
- Incentivize your fans with a referral program or loyalty program.

Hypothesis 2: Improve buyer experience by removing last-minute objections

Video landing pages, also known as lead capture pages, static pages, destination pages, or post-click pages, are a specific way of using video on your website. They can feature a video as the centerpiece of the page or include it alongside text and other rich media below the fold to help convince visitors to buy. (Vidyard, 2020)[159]

Videos allow visitors to experience your message with little effort beyond an initial click. They also let you convey ideas that images, copy, and animation cannot - and they do it in a universally compelling format. (Unbounce, 2019)[160]

There are a few different ways you can use videos on a landing page (Vidyard, 2020)[161]:

- Hero Landing Page Video: Replaces a standard hero image at the top of your landing page or is otherwise featured as the primary visual above-the-fold
- Supporting Landing Page Video: Appears lower down, below-the-fold, on the page as a supporting asset.
- Background Landing Page Video: Serves as an animated background to draw attention to the headline, a key piece of text, a button, or a form
- Lightbox Landing Page Video: Opens in a lightbox popup to play after the viewer clicks a link, button, or thumbnail.

Nearly all video platforms allow some form of embedding, provided that these are public videos.

If traffic generation and lead conversion are your goals, use platforms like Wistia. They are designed precisely with that in mind.

Hypothesis 3: Remove friction by offering an in-video buying experience

When a video's call-to-action is to buy something, it usually implies that the viewer needs to leave the video environment for a sales platform, such as a Shopify store, or to one of your owned media assets, a landing page, for example. In the process, a lot of potential customers get cold feet and abort the buying process.

A way to avoid this is to offer a solution that allows you to sell without leaving the video platform.

Traditional e-commerce has been growing for years, but the pandemic increased its momentum. In the US alone, online shopping's share of total retail sales grew 44% in 2020.[162] According to a report by DemandGen, 86% of buyers now prefer interactive, visual content that can be accessed on-demand. (DemandGen, 2019)[163]

But what exactly do they mean when they say "interactive"?

Shoppable videos feature products and use embedded links to enable viewers to click and purchase those products instantly without leaving the video. They allow brands to replicate the experience of visiting their website without the consumer having to leave the social platform they're enjoying. (ChannelSight, 2021)[164]

How do shoppable videos work? Viewers can click on the custom call to action buttons with embedded links to instantly purchase products without leaving the platform. This allows customers to contact the brands and purchase products directly from the video.

- Shoppable videos on YouTube complement your ad with browsable product imagery to inspire the next purchase. All you need to do is sync your Google Merchant Center feed to your video ads, and you can visually expand your call-to-action button with the bestsellers you want to feature and drive traffic to the product pages that matter. (Google Ads & Commerce Blog, 2020)[165]

- Shoppable videos on Instagram are primarily available on Stories, with Instagram offering to fill out your name, address, and connected credit card.
- In-app purchases on TikTok: From the TikTok app, you can create Conversion Ads directly on Shopify. This will allow you to create ads that will drive valuable actions on your Shopify store. (TikTok Business Help Center)[166]

This process is often described as Social Commerce. Social Commerce is a subset of e-commerce that involves social media and online media that supports social interaction and user contributions to assist online buying and selling products and services.

Livestream shopping combines livestreaming with the ability to buy products directly via the Livestream. It is an emerging trend that offers consumers a more engaging experience than simply clicking and filling a virtual shopping cart. (InfluencerMarketingHub, 2021)[167]

In the West, 49% of online shoppers say they would buy products directly from live videos where brands, celebrities, or influencers they follow are launching new products. (GFK for Facebook for Business, 2020)[168]

According to Google, one reason for this preference for Livestream shopping is that while consumers want the convenience of researching and reviewing products online at home, they also wish the trusted guidance of an in-store experience.[169]

Customers like Livestream shopping because the experience allows them to get to know, like, and trust the vendors before deciding to buy.

Livestream shopping is still in its infancy in countries like the UK and the USA. In China, however, it's a booming industry.[170]

Taobao, China's largest online marketplace, reported that between 2018 and 2021, livestreaming would provide them with over 500 billion transactions. In 2018 no more than 81 influencers generated $15m+ in sales through livestreaming.

Cheri opened her first Taobao shop (Chinshop) when she was still a college student.

2.2.4 CUSTOMERS STOP USING YOUR SERVICE

*Canadian musician Dave Carroll's song "United Breaks Guitars" was released in 2009
and became an immediate hit on YouTube (and a PR disaster for United Airlines).*

Not every disgruntled customer will put a video online to vent their frustrations. But the mere fact that they make this effort points to a much larger underlying issue. By the time unhappy customers take to social media or review sites to complain, they probably have already tried to contact the business but were dissatisfied with the response (or the lack thereof).

Customer satisfaction plays an essential role within your business (About Calls, 2017)[171]:

1   It is the leading indicator to measure customer loyalty, identify unhappy customers, reduce churn and increase revenue;

2   It is a crucial point of differentiation that helps you to attract new customers in competitive business environments.

Ignoring these complaints will hurt your business: potential customers in the consideration phase will stumble upon these negative reviews and will change their minds about buying from you. Never ignore an unhappy customer. There's no un-ringing the negative publicity bell. (Patel, 2017)[172]

The relationship between an organization and its customers doesn't end with the purchase. That's where the whole relationship takes off! You should focus this relationship on customer loyalty.

When a customer is loyal to one company, they aren't easily swayed by price or availability. They would rather pay more and ensure the same quality service and product they know and love. (NiceReply, 2020)[173]

Customers who trust the companies they do business with will be more likely to purchase again in the future. And if you're lucky, they'll also recommend your service to their friends and family.

Like all relationships, customer loyalty doesn't happen overnight. You win your customers over with exceptional customer service, support, commitment, and empathy. Show, don't tell that you're willing to go the extra mile for your customers – this will reassure potential buyers at the beginning of their buyer journey.

Video marketing is a powerful tool to convince customers through the more classic tactics to stimulate customer loyalty, either by reminding them to renew their subscription, sharing the brand's history, or promoting a new product. (ClipChamp, 2020)[174]

Creating an emotional bond between you and your audience can bring you repeat business and indefinite brand loyalty. This is where videos come in: videos work at a different emotional level.

Video is the perfect way to deliver quicker and more effective solutions to customer woes. It speeds up the resolution process. It makes customers happier with their support experience. It even boosts customer retention by helping them get more out of your product or service. (Vidyard, 2020)[175]

Take, for example, customer care. Some questions by customers are Frequently Asked Questions.

Research the most googled question and make a video with the answer. Create a series of unlisted videos that answer those Frequently Asked Questions and use these to answer customer questions by email.

Sometimes customer satisfaction is guaranteed with something as simple as a "Thank you for your purchase."

 A warm and welcoming thank you video on the order confirmation page is a powerful way to improve customer loyalty and retention.

Thank you videos show business owners expressing their gratitude to their consumers. People love feeling appreciated, valued, and thanked. Plus, it gives customers a chance to look at the human face behind a business. You can be creative with your thank you videos, especially during the holidays, and wish them a short and simple "Happy Thanksgiving," a "Merry Christmas," or a "Happy New Year."

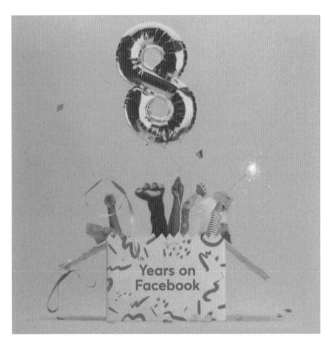

Facebook "Faceversary" Personalized Video.

2.2.5   **NOBODY SPONTANEOUSLY RECOMMENDS YOU**

THE BENDY TRIPOD
3,728,133 views • Jul 5, 2016   👍 88K   👎 1.4K   ➔ SHARE   ≡₊ SAVE   ...

In 2016, vlogger Casey Neistat uploaded a vlog titled "THE BENDY TRIPOD" recommending the JOBY GorillaPod tripod.

Brand advocacy (customers spontaneously recommending your brand) is the pot of gold at the end of the rainbow. Brand advocacy can be an effective way of increasing the reach of your company. This process involves finding people who prefer your products and services. Finding these customers is essential because they might be willing to promote your brand to new customers. (ScholarlyYOA, 2021)[176]

Hypothesis 1: Create videos that people will want to share

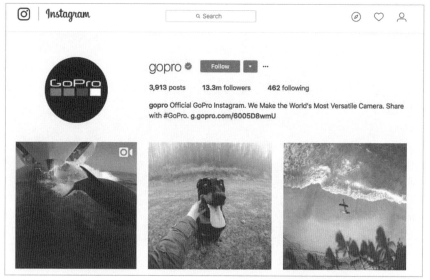

GoPro uses Instagram to post videos taken using their cameras regularly.

Will your customers spontaneously share your videos or create videos to recommend your products to their audience? Probably not. But the least you can do is to make it easy and attractive for them to do so.

Hypothesis 2: Reshare User Generated Content

How do you find your brand advocates? Through social media listening. Remember: natural brand advocates are happy customers, so they will go to the effort of mentioning your account name in their post.

How do you incentivize your brand advocates? By resharing their user-generated content. This is called retweet on Twitter and reshare on Instagram.

 Make sure you mention the original poster! Usually, corporate accounts have more followers than regular users. The reward for them is that this reshare will increase their reach, resulting in more followers.

2.3 FIND YOUR CONTENT FOCUS

Congratulations! You have now identified your video marketing strategy. What is the next step?

It's very tempting to go straight to your choice of video formats, like a daily vlog on YouTube or a series of behind-the-scenes videos on Instagram. But you would be skipping a crucial element in your marketing strategy: defining your content focus (or niche, as some video producers like to call it).

Your content focus is the "point of concentration." It's the specialized section or category you create your content around. Your focus is what you are examining, discussing, illuminating, sharing, or conveying. (Deziel, 2020)[177]

 Always start with the focus, and then determine which format is best suited to the story you want to tell. (Deziel, 2020)[178]

Why not go for a blanket "everything for everybody" video strategy?

 Cosmically big topics will not lead to a larger audience. Start your research with a broad issue, study the channels for this topic and learn from them what works and what doesn't. Then find your angle for this topic or add your twist.

Have the confidence to find your niche, define who you are, then declare it again and again and again and again. If you do it persistently enough, you will own that niche. People will not be able to imagine that niche without you. (Sivers, 2020)[179]

Why start only with one particular content focus for your first series of consistent topic videos? They help you build momentum and traction with your audience, so they keep coming back for more. Once your reach is broad enough, you can still branch off into other related topics. If they stick, continue on that road.

Examples:

- Horror movie reviews in Dutch
- Space exploration for children
- Vegan baking for people who can't cook (and won't cook)

Don't get blinded by the total amount of views on other people's videos. YouTube and TikTok total views don't take time into account.

What you're seeing is the current, successful stage of their video journey. Your journey will be different! Instead, see what you can learn from their process, their experiments, and their mistakes.

 If you're struggling to find an identity or purpose for your YouTube channel, build it at the intersection of your passion, your proficiency, and your profit. (Cannell & Travis, 2018)[180]

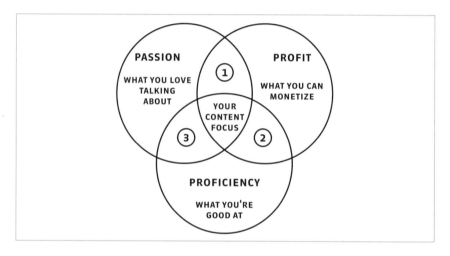

Ikigai for video marketing

Note: The original Japanese Ikigai philosophy didn't include the Profit part. Initially, working out your Ikigai meant finding the "sweet spot" between what you loved, what you were good at, and what the world needed.

It's ok if you don't find your content focus immediately.

1   If you are passionate about what you make videos about, and there's a way to make money from them, then it's ok if the production value of your videos is not that high. Authenticity > perfection

2   It's perfectly possible to make videos that bring in revenue and that are professionally made. But if your heart is not in it, I recommend outsourcing it to a professional video producer.

3   If you're passionate about your content focus, and you're good at making attractive videos about it, then it's perfectly normal if, at first, you're not making any money with it. Winning your audience's trust takes time.

Passion

Write a list of things you're passionate about:

- When you do these, time flies by.
- You would do it, even if you didn't get paid for it.

 Don't go for the "I'm passionate about food/travel" clichés. Everybody loves good food. And everybody loves going on holiday. Dig deeper.

- If your day-to-day responsibilities were taken care of and you could throw yourself completely behind a cause, what would it be?
- What charities do you support, and why?
- What nonprofit organizations do you support?
- You're gathering signatures for a petition - what's your cause?

Profit

Passion is what got you started. But passion doesn't pay your bills. Customers do.

Will your audience be attractive to advertisers? Will it be attractive enough to build a business on?

 An easy way to find how "monetizable" a topic can be is to look in your Google Adsense account. You can search for keywords related to the topic, and Google will tell you the average cost per click for ads. Topics and keywords with a higher cost will mean YouTube channels related to those topics serving ads will make more money.

So can you earn a living selling video content online? Yes. Chase your focus, mission, passion, and purpose, and allow money and income to stem from that. (Cannell & Travis, 2018)[181]

There are three ways to make money from your videos:

1   Via the video platform

2   From your community

3   By monetizing your video skills

 See also Chapter 4.6 Monetize your skills

Proficiency

Proficiency is not just about video production skills. It also involves being able to add real value to your target audience. What do you do better than all the others in the field?

No camera or editing skills? No problem. You can build that airplane on your way down. Publish when you have time; your audience watches when they have time. Then, when your videos have gained traction and momentum, focus on high production value.

 See also Chapter 3 Run – shoot, upload and promote your videos

2.4 MATCH WITH CONTENT FORMATS

Now that we've defined our content focus, we can select a format (or multiple formats) by asking ourselves, "What is the best way to bring this story to life?" (Deziel, 2020)[182]

2.4.1 LIVE-ACTION OR ANIMATED?

Live-action is a form of cinematography or videography that uses photography instead of animation. Some works combine live-action with animation to create a live-action animated film. Some examples of live-action videos are:

- Behind-the-scenes videos
- Talking-head videos

A talking-head video is where the main action involves someone just talking to the camera, either right into it or slightly to the side, interview style. To be clear, there is nothing inherently wrong with a video of a person talking to the camera. (Tendo, 2018)[183] Some examples of talking-head videos are:

- Vlogs
- Webinars or presentations
- Testimonials, customer interviews, and case studies
- Q&A and AMA sessions
- Guest interviews / Talk show / Podcast recording session
- Product reviews

A video blog, sometimes shortened to vlog, is a blog for which the medium is video. Vlogs have magic to them that other video formats don't have. The vlog category is popular on the video-sharing platform YouTube.

[Vlogs] are those in-depth teenage conversations behind locked bedroom doors so that your parents don't hear; they're the snatched discussions in nightclub bathrooms before heading back out onto the dance floor; they're stepping into the confession booth as the priest, sitting down and hearing the person on the other side pouring out their heart and soul. (Stokel-Walker, 2018)[184]

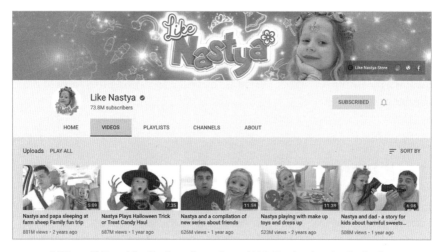

Millions of kids and families from all over the world join Russian-Amerian family vlog Like Nastya every day to explore the world and learn about songs, numbers, nature, colors, shapes, animals, and the importance of eating healthy food, washing hands, being a good friend, and much more.

Common categories for vlogs are:

- Entertainment videos
- Reaction videos
- Roundup videos

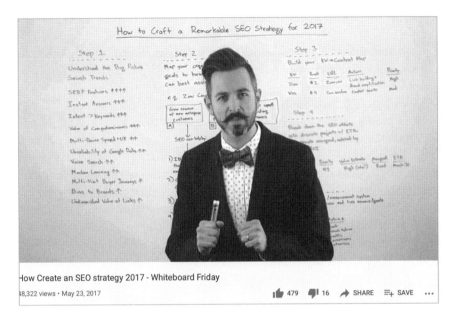

How Create an SEO strategy 2017 - Whiteboard Friday

8,322 views • May 23, 2017   👍 479   👎 16   ➔ SHARE   ⊒₊ SAVE   ...

Don't have a fancy recording studio? As Rand Fishkin did with his "Whiteboard Friday"
movies for Moz, turn your limitations into an opportunity.

Not all marketing videos have to feature humans (or even animals). If it's not a "live-action" video, it often features a voice-over or a soundtrack.

A few examples:

- Slides shows or carousels
- Explainer videos & how-to videos
- Product demos
- Animation videos

2.4.2   LIVE OR ON-DEMAND?

On-demand videos feature videos that were pre-recorded. They are a safe choice, which makes them perfect for:

- More formal presentations and webinars.
- New product launch videos.
- Sales videos for clients.

Facebook Watch, launched in 2018, is Facebook's video-on-demand service that combines aspects of its video-sharing functionality with premium content. It allows creators to upload their own short- and long-form videos, including original comedy, drama, and news comedy.

Humans of New York: The Series is one of Facebook Watch's Originals.

Social media platforms want you to stay on their turf for as long as possible. Never post a link to YouTube on Facebook or LinkedIn. Upload natively instead.

Native video is video content uploaded directly to (or created on) a social network and played in-feed on that platform. For example, on Facebook, a native video would be a video that is uploaded directly to Facebook rather than a link shared from Youtube or Vimeo. (Biteable)[185]

Livestreaming is an exciting way to connect with your audience in real-time. Livestreaming refers to online streaming media simultaneously recorded and broadcast in real-time. It is often referred to as streaming, but this abbreviated term is ambiguous because "streaming" may refer to any media delivered and played back simultaneously without requiring a completely downloaded file.

You can use live videos to:

- Answer questions,
- Respond to comments, or
- Just generally build a sense of camaraderie.

 Consider doing long broadcasts (perhaps one to two hours), as it gives your audience a greater chance to join your video.

Nintendo uses YouTube livestreams to speak directly to its customers, delivering news and product updates.

During the pandemic, livestreaming technology enabled closed venues to continue to reach their audience.

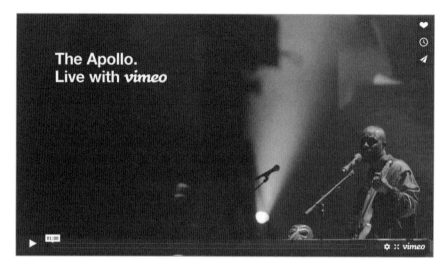

New York's historic Apollo Theater kicked off their 2020 fall season with a virtual concert featuring Wyclef Jean.[186]

Pros of livestreaming:

- Most livestreams can be recorded by anyone who is broadcasting. These recorded events are gifts that keep giving since you can use the recordings as on-demand content after the actual live event is over.
- In terms of expenses, it's less expensive than the production and editing costs of a pre-recorded video for your business. (Wistia, 2021)[187]

Cons of livestreaming:

- Murphy's Law very much applies to livestreaming. When a Livestream gets interrupted, all you can do is hope your audience keeps trying to reconnect.

 It's painful for an audience to watch speakers grappling with a tech problem, so have graphics or video ready that say something along the lines of, "We are experiencing technical issues – please stand by."

Most popular social media platforms allow for live broadcasting by individuals and businesses.

Note: Twitter officially shut down its livestreaming feature in March 2021. I wouldn't be surprised if they tried to reenter this space at some point, but you'll have to stick to other platforms for your streams for now.

The most notable livestreaming platforms are Facebook Live, YouTube Live, Vimeo Live, and, of course, Twitch.

Most Twitch streamers seem to prefer Open Broadcast Software. Open Broadcaster Software (OBS) is a free, open-source streaming and video recording program. You can obtain OBS Studio from the OBS Project website. It is multi-platform, working on Windows, Mac, and Linux. obsproject.com

If you want to cast a wide net, multi-destination streaming might be an option.

Multistreaming means going live to multiple platforms, like Facebook, YouTube, and LinkedIn, simultaneously. It offers serious benefits like an increased reach. When you go live to another platform, you're exposing a whole new audience to your content. And, if done effectively, it can essentially multiply your viewership. (Streamyard)[188]

There are several solutions for multistreaming.

Use a combination of hardware (e.g., Mevo camera) and online video services (e.g., Vimeo Pro Plan). This has the added benefit of managing the camera shots from the Mevo app on your smartphone. You're mobile, which means you can multistream from anywhere!

Use specialized software as a service from your desktop. This works perfectly with external video and audio sources (e.g., a DSLR camera and lavalier microphones) in a studio environment. The most popular multistream software solutions are Restream.io and Streamyard.

Complete your desktop streaming software with, for example, a hardware keyboard to manage multicamera input. Some examples are Elgato's Stream Deck or Cam Link 4K, Blackmagicdesign's Atem Mini, or Rode's RØDECaster Pro.

Your choice of software also depends upon:

1   The destinations of your stream, and

2   The video features you'd like to use in real-time.

- Overlay graphics (transparent or full screen): visuals and animated text to convey your message or show your logo
- Lower thirds, for example, a ticker
- Include pre-recorded video clips in the stream
- The talking head can share their computer screen
- The audience can interact with chat or video

 If you want to have professional features similar to those of a T.V. broadcasting studio, consider vMix. vMix is a complete live video production software solution with features including live mixing, switching, recording and livestreaming of SD, full HD and 4K video sources including cameras, video files, DVDs, images, Powerpoint and much much more.

Want to know more?

- Twitch Broadcasting Guidelines stream.twitch.tv
- YouTube live:
  - YouTube Digital Events Playbook[189]
  - Creator Academy Learning Toolkit. Learn the basics of getting started with livestreaming and best practices, including features and setup tips, that can help you take your next Livestream to the next level.[190]
- Facebook For Media Tips for using Facebook Live[191]
- Vimeo Livestream Events Guide vimeo.com/enterprise/livestream-event-guide

HORIZONTAL OR VERTICAL VIDEO?

No doubt you've come across videos that seem cut off on the sides or the top. Or, worse, the video platform fills up the screen's real estate with black rectangles or blurred images. This happens when creators don't use the correct aspect ratios for the videos when uploading them to the platform.

An aspect ratio is a number that encompasses how wide or how high your video is. It's the proportional relationship between a video's width and height. (Wistia blog, 2019)[192]

The most common aspect ratios for digital videos are:

- 1:1 = square video
- 16:9 = landscape video
- 9:16 = portrait video

The default aspect ratio of your footage is defined by the type of camera you use, for example:

- DSLR shoots in 16:9 aspect ratio by default
- Cameraphones are usually held in portrait mode when recording video.

How can you avoid getting your video mangled because its aspect ratio doesn't fit the requirements of the video platform you uploaded it to?

There are two ways:

1   Export your video in the format that best fits the platform you upload it to. Some editing formats allow for this type of export. The video format templates offered by tools like canva.com and lumen5.com can save you a lot of time!

2   Align elements towards the center of your screen. Like other social media platforms, Instagram crops content to try to optimize it as much as possible. (Influencer Marketing Hub, 2021)[193]

For the "older" video and video marketing platforms, landscape video orientation (16:9) is still the standard:

- Vimeo
- YouTube
- Wistia
- Twitch

Upload horizontal videos, and they'll reformat when the viewer turns their phone or work both horizontally or vertically (more or less).

Mobile-first social media platforms like TikTok and Snapchat have portrait mode (9:16) as their default. This also goes for (Video) Stories, which was practically invented by Snapchat but later copied by Facebook, Instagram, and even LinkedIn.

But then it gets weird.

- Facebook video can be anything between landscape (16:9) and portrait (9:16).
- LinkedIn video can be landscape (16:9), square (1:1), or portrait (9:16).
- Instagram allows for landscape (16:9 – especially for IGTV), square (1:1), and, weirdly enough, an "almost square" video format with a 4:5 aspect ratio.
- Twitter video is square (1:1 aspect ratio)
- Pinterest video pins are a hot mess with 1:1, 2:3, 4:5, or 9:16 aspect ratios.
- Don't get me started about Instagram Reels or YouTube Shorts.

When these social media platforms offer video ads, they mostly follow the recommended sizes for their regular videos.

All the big social media platforms are coalescing in format by liberally borrowing each other's innovations. They are seeking a straightforward thing: what works in driving traffic and all-important dwell time. Open up any big video and photo sharing platforms – whether Facebook, Instagram, Snapchat, or YouTube – and they look increasingly alike. (Stokel-Walker, 2018)[194]

 Choose from the start whether your video will be published in horizontal or in vertical mode. Going for both results in videos might feel "off" in some circumstances.

Pros of horizontal video:

- Horizontal is perfect for storytelling. In theater, new elements are most often introduced on the left side of the stage. As they push the story forward, they move from left to right. This left-to-right movement still feels natural for actions in storytelling.
- A horizontal shot allows both participants to be visible in interview settings whether they're speaking or not.
- The word "horizon" gives it away: horizontal is perfect for filming landscapes or seascapes.
- If the video features a talking head, the horizontal mode offers more real estate combined with a shared computer screen, a picture-in-picture, or a leader board.

Pros of vertical video:

- Since regular people on their phones film it, vertical videos are perceived as more authentic.
- Vertical videos are perfect when filming one person moving without taking up a lot of the floor space. Example: models showcasing fashion items on Instagram or TikTok.
- Vertical videos are the default for mobile-first video platforms and ephemeral media like Stories (that disappear 24 hours).

Mobile videos are often watched sneakily (for example, during boring meetings) or by people on the go. In both cases, they want to watch discreetly and with the sound turned off.

Whether your audience has their sound on or off, you should create your video to be effective with and without sound. If you have something to say, use captions. But keep them short. Challenge yourself to communicate your key message using only imagery.

Use some of these techniques to captivate your sound-off audience (Facebook Blueprint course):[195]

- Use visual elements to tell your story and highlight what matters.
- Incorporate animation, text overlays, graphics, or captions, and subtitles.
- Add stacking type to bring viewers into your story.
- Use overlays to add texture and dimension to your videos.

2.5 SELECT THE PROPER VIDEO CHANNELS

Only now is it time to select the right "home" for your videos. Where will the videos live? It's pointless producing a video without considering its purpose. While some videos are for ad campaigns, others are for websites, YouTube channels, blog posts, social media pages, or product pages on Amazon.

Be careful not to pick a video marketing channel only because of assumptions about its audience's demographics.

E.g. Instagram is for millennials.

However, millennials indeed use Instagram and YouTube more than respondents as a whole and other age groups. But the Instagram demographic is much more mainstream now.

E.g. Nobody uses Facebook anymore.

Facebook is still popular with older millennials and up. Facebook is King of the 40+ demographic!

E.g. TikTok is for Gen Z.

TikTok may be popular with under 25-year-olds, but there's increasing evidence that its users are growing with TikTok instead of abandoning it as they grow older. That means TikTok users who start at 16 or 18 do not give up the app when they turn 20. (Influencer MarketingHub, 2020)

E.g. American users have left TikTok.

When the US announced that they might ban TikTok, many creators started diversifying towards YouTube and Instagram. But most stayed loyal to the platform. TikTok is still banned in India, however.

 Start with a maximum of three channels and do those well. Each year, replace the least performing one with a promising newcomer.

Overview of video-first platforms

	VIMEO	YOUTUBE	WISTIA	TWITCH	TIKTOK
Video first?	Yes	Yes	Yes	Yes	Yes
Native video available since?	2004	2005	2006	2011	2016
Discovery feed?	No	Yes	No	No	Yes
Considered as social media?	No	No	No	No	No
Video ads?	No	Yes	No	Yes	Yes

Overview of other video-enabled platforms

	INSTAGRAM	SNAPCHAT	TWITTER	FACEBOOK	LINKEDIN	PINTEREST
Video first?	No	No	No	No	No	No
Native video available since?	2013	2014	2015	2017	2017	2020
Discovery feed?	Yes	No	Yes	Yes	Yes	Yes
Considered as social media?	Yes	Yes	Yes	Yes	Yes	Yes
Video ads?	Yes	No	Yes	Yes	Yes	Yes

2.5.1   YOUTUBE

YouTube is an online video platform owned by Google. It is the second most-visited website in the world. YouTube is the largest video-first platform; it is also the second-most used social network (after Facebook). YouTube is the number two search engine in the world (behind Google).

YouTube is massive, global, and key to building relevancy with audiences of all ages, with interests ranging from comedy, sports, fashion, gaming, food, or simply everyday life. YouTube may have gained popularity as a platform for personal video viewing, but it has also been a valuable marketing machine. But its biggest asset is that YouTube is a place where people watch videos with intention.

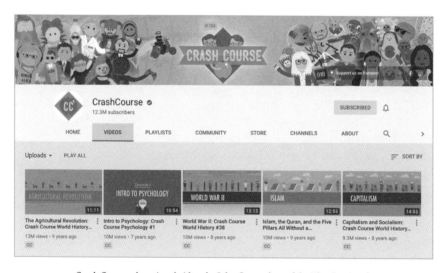

Crash Course educational videos by John Greene (one of the Vlog Brothers).

 Humor is highly subjective, and there's no guarantee that you have what it takes to make someone else laugh. If you try to be funny and no one laughs, you end up with one terrible video. (Miller 2008)[196]

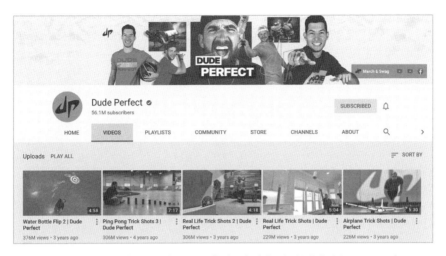

Dude Perfect YouTube channel consists of "5 best buds just kickin' it," mixing sports and comedy in entertaining ways.

 YouTube automatically generates captions for each uploaded video. This means that you can download a ready-made captions file for each video – a script with time codes. Download the captions file (in SRT or VTT format), then upload alongside your video on Facebook or LinkedIn, for example, or import the file in a professional editing program. (Trip, 2020)[197]

YouTube is different from a traditional media company: its reach is more expansive, its diversity broader, its demographic younger, and its power stronger. YouTube is a kaleidoscope of visual and audio content that mimics the richness, quirkiness, beauty, and madness of human life. (Stokel-Walker, 2018)[198]

For any type of business, YouTube is a powerful marketing machine. People are already on YouTube searching for answers and things they are interested in. Providing content that is helpful or valuable to an audience can potentially gain traction over time.

YouTube videos are also an SEO shortcut: if a how-to YouTube video is the best answer to someone's Google query, it will rank very high in search results. YouTube videos are beneficial for SEO and help a product or brand to start ranking higher for search terms relative to the product or industry.

Although it's straightforward to set up a YouTube channel, the hard part is to keep working on it and posting regularly to increase subscribers and keep your audience engaged.

+ Want to know more?

- YouTube Creator Academy creatoracademy.youtube.com

2.5.2 TIKTOK

TikTok, known in China as Douyin, is a video-sharing social networking service owned by Chinese company ByteDance. The social media app is used to make a variety of short-form videos, from genres like dance, comedy, and education, with a duration of 15 seconds to one minute.

TikTok is the leading destination for short-form mobile video and is very popular with younger generations.

Popular topics on TikTok are challenges, dance videos, karaoke, reaction videos, dialogue reenactments, and cute animal videos.

In 2019, Charli D'Amelio from Connecticut rocketed to the top of TikTok in just a matter of months through choreographed dances to viral songs.

If you are a young dancer, musician, comedienne, actress, or magician, you should get on TikTok as quickly as possible to take advantage of the app's one billion users to grow your brand/business. TikTok raises new Internet celebrities and micro-influencers every day, and the number of people who have become hugely successful entertainers because of the platform is nearly endless. (Olson, 2020)[199]

During the 2020 lockdown, The Washington Post gave one of their contributors free rein over their TikTok, resulting in slightly absurd, funny, and endearing videos.

In 2020, established celebrities and experts flocked to the platform to participate in the direct interaction and as an easy way to express creativity.

Famous chef Gordon Ramsay enjoys responding (stitching) to cooking videos to give his comments in his well-known, slightly abrasive style.

TikTok is rapidly expanding to different categories and demographics. Due to the nature of the algorithm, people see similar content to what they watch entirely and interact with. These unofficial connections are often referred to by the topic followed by "-tok". Quite a lot of creators are known for their particular issues and collaboration.

Examples are StockTok about investing, LawyerTok about legal matters, and QueerTok about all LGBTQ+ issues. This has attracted a lot of niche creators who typically are experts in their field. Academics, plastic surgeons, NASA scientists, cooks...

Fashion brands like Gucci, Urban Outfitters, Nike, or FashionNova connect with
their audience on TikTok.

Popular topics: Comedy sketches, music and dance, microblogs, education.

2.5.3 VIMEO

Vimeo is an American video hosting, sharing, and services platform that launched in 2004. Vimeo describes itself as "The world's leading all-in-one video solution" and focuses on the delivery of high-definition video across a range of devices. Vimeo's business model is through software as a service, starting with a free plan and premium subscriptions available to unlock powerful tools.

The most significant advantage of Vimeo over YouTube or Facebook is that Vimeo offers a minimal and clean viewing experience. There are no ads or other suggested videos at the end of your video and you have more embedding options, like disabling fullscreen or hiding the video controls. Today, Vimeo is the world's largest ad-free open video platform. Its video software provides powerful tools to host, share and sell videos in the highest quality possible.

This is why most of Vimeo's reported 200 million users are part of the filmmaking and storytelling community. Its main feature is that the platform allows professionals from the creative industry to showcase their videos in "Stunning 4K Ultra HD".

Vimeo is a good home for your videos with higher production value. Vimeo also acts as a publishing tool for social platforms (Facebook Pages, YouTube, Twitter, LinkedIn Company Pages, Pinterest, and Shopify Product Pages).

Vimeo relies on strategic partnerships to empower more businesses and marketers to succeed with video. "Powered by Vimeo" partnerships include integrations with Constant Contact, GoDaddy, Shopify, Facebook, Eventbrite, Pinterest, and Patreon.

 Want to know more?

- Video for Business vimeo.com/blog/category/video-for-business

2.5.4   WISTIA

Wistia was founded in 2006 in Cambridge, Massachusetts, by two university friends. The company makes marketing software, video series, and educational content based on "the belief that anyone can use video to grow their business and their brand."

Wistia is not a social platform but video marketing software that marketers can use to find, engage and grow their audience.

The platform has powerful video SEO and tools for creating smarter ads on search and social media. Wistia is great for marketers because it offers integrations with standard sales and marketing tools like Hubspot, Marketo, and Pardot. Like Vimeo, Wistia can also be used as a way to publish videos to social channels.

Wistia does a great job of educating small businesses on making better videos – from being on camera to explaining what gear you need.

Want to know more?

- Wistia Guide to Video Marketing wistia.com/about/video-marketing-guide

2.5.5 TWITCH

Twitch is an American video livestreaming service owned by Amazon.com. Introduced in June 2011 as a spin-off of the general-interest streaming platform Justin.tv, the site primarily focuses on video game livestreaming, broadcasts of esports competitions, music broadcasts, creative content, and more recently, "in real life" streams.

Twitch thrives on livestreams and interaction with the chat. This is an excellent way for brands to interact with the community, answer questions, or make announcements.

American Twitch streamer Ludwig "Ludwig" Ahlgren is best known
for his livestreams on Twitch.

Twitch is best for exclusive shows, scheduled repeating format, showing something with commentary and interaction with the chat. Gaming, art, and slice of life content are prevalent.

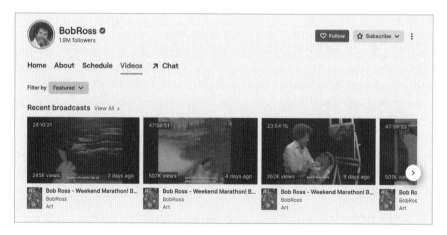

Fans of American art instructor Bob Ross join every week for the weekend marathons on Twitch that begin every Friday at 12PM EDT. This marathon replays episodes of Bob Ross' famous "The Joy of Painting" T.V. series that became the most watched painting program in the world.

Amazon is the ultimate owner of Twitch, the livestreaming website best known for hosting some of the world's most significant gamers – but it takes a hands-off approach to run the site. Twitch has recently made moves to increase the proportion of 'IRL' (non-gaming) streams on its site. If that sounds a bit like YouTube to you, that's because it is. (Stokel-Walker, 2018)[200]

Want to know more?

- Twitch Advertising twitchadvertising.tv

2.5.6 **INSTAGRAM VIDEO**

Instagram is "a simple, fun & creative way to capture, edit & share photos, videos & messages with friends & family." Instagram launched native video in 2016.

Like Facebook, Instagram is not a platform for hosting videos, but it allows you to connect with and grow an audience through location tags, hashtags, stories, livestreams, and influencers.

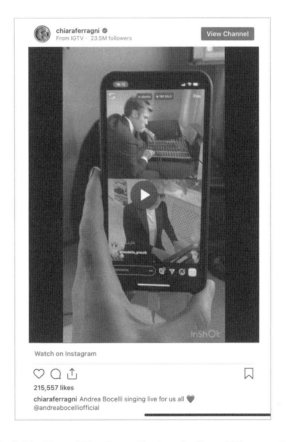

Italian fashion blogger Chiara Ferragni has tens of millions of followers on IGTV.

IGTV (Instagram TV) complements Instagram Stories and enables accounts to create long-form vertical video content. Think of it as a vertical YouTube for an Instagram audience.

✚ Want to know more?

- Get Started with Instagram business.instagram.com
- Using Video on Instagram (Facebook for Business, 2016)[201]
- Ultimate Guide to Instagram Video (Later, 2020)[202]
- Instagram Video: A Complete Guide (Animoto, 2019)[203]
- Instagram Video: Best Practices and Tools for Creating Engaging Content (Hootsuite, 2021)[204]
- The Ultimate Guide to Instagram for Business in 2021 (Oberlo, 2021)[205]

2.5.7 **FACEBOOK VIDEO**

Native video on Facebook, the largest social media platform, was launched in 2017. While you can share videos from other platforms to Facebook, native videos (video files uploaded directly to Facebook) are favored by the algorithm.

 Document your startup's story through Facebook video stories and even host live Q&As through Facebook Live to start having conversations in real-time with future and existing customers.

The primary activity of Facebook users is "Keeping in touch with friends and family," but sharing videos is part of the social fabric. Facebook's video ecosystem currently includes Messenger, WhatsApp, Instagram, Oculus, and more. However, the platform's video ambitions failed to get out of the shadows cast by video giants YouTube and TikTok.

This didn't stop Facebook from becoming the largest platform for video advertising. Facebook (including Instagram) has a 50-60% share of online video display advertising and a 40-50% share of online non-video display advertising. (YouTube is the second largest supplier in video display advertising, with a 15-20% share of expenditure.) (CMA, 2020)[206]

Facebook is also opening the door to short-form content through integration with Instagram Reels. Facebook is also incentivizing short-form content creation across markets. The company announced in March 2021 that it would begin offering creators revenue for short-form video and states: "We're especially focused on short-form video monetization."

Facebook famously doesn't have a thumbs down button. Popular topics include comedy, education, feel-good content, and pets and animals.

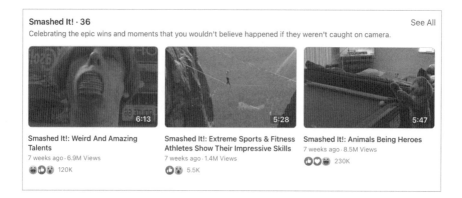

LADbible is a UK news and entertainment brand, created for the youth community.
Their video uploads are among the most popular on the Facebook platform.

✚ Want to know more?

- Facebook for Business: How to make a video for Facebook[207]
- About Video (Facebook For Business – Business Help Center)[208]
- Facebook Blueprint Course: Video Best Practices Checklist[209]
- Facebook for Media: Understanding How Your Videos Perform on Facebook[210]

2.5.8   **SNAPCHAT VIDEO**

Snapchat, initially released in 2011, is a mobile app for Android and iOS devices that "lets you easily talk with friends, view Live Stories from around the world, and explore news in Discover."

Snapchat's tragic fate is that innovative social media features like Stories were first introduced by them, only to be later copied by tech giants like Facebook and Instagram. Back in 2015, Snapchat's developers realized that it might be the social video, not the photo, that would become the standard unit of image speak. (Brennan, 2020)[211] These social videos are now the secret to TikTok's success. TikTok provides people with entertainment from strangers, while Snapchat connects friends.

This doesn't stop Snapchat from continuing to drive technological innovation. Right now, Snapchat's video filters are a prime example of AR/VR Immersive media that mix real-world objects and people with virtual ones, closing the gap between reality and virtuality. "Augmented Reality (AR) experiences that let you step inside scenes of your favorite shows or videos; AR experiences that let you experience video from all angles and get up close and personal with your favorite personalities or characters." (Snap, 2020)[212]

 Want to know more?

- Snapchat for Business forbusiness.snapchat.com

2.5.9 TWITTER VIDEO

Twitter is an American microblogging and social networking service on which users post and interact with messages known as "tweets." Registered users can post, like, and retweet tweets, but unregistered users can only read them. Twitter launched native video in 2015. Today, Twitter describes itself as "an open service that's home to a world of diverse people, perspectives, ideas, and information." (About Twitter)[213]

Twitter acquired American social networking short-form video hosting service Vine in 2012, only to discontinue this service in 2016. Periscope was an American live video streaming app for Android and iOS acquired by Twitter before launch in 2015. In 2020, Twitter announced that Periscope, its livestreaming service, would shut down on March 31st, 2021.[214]

✚ Want to know more?

- Twitter Business business.twitter.com

2.5.10 LINKEDIN VIDEO

LinkedIn was founded in 2002, which makes it one of the oldest surviving social media platforms. The LinkedIn mission statement is to "connect the world's professionals to make them more productive and successful."

In August 2017, LinkedIn launched native video to its users. Inspired by what had been used on Facebook for the previous couple of years, LinkedIn rolled out this new video posting capability on LinkedIn globally to increase in-feed engagement and boost the platform's usability. The video feature is particularly interesting for B2B marketers. One year later, brands could also leverage video for Sponsored Content and Company Pages.

Motivational speaker and best selling author Simon Sinek started recording short videos to LinkedIn when his speaking gigs got cancelled because of the 2020 pandemic.

➕ Want to know more?

- LinkedIn Marketing Solutions: Video Ads[215]
- Everything You Need to Know About LinkedIn Video (Hootsuite, 2021)[216]

2.5.11 PINTEREST VIDEO PINS

American image sharing and social media service Pinterest was founded in 2010. Pinterest describes itself as "a visual discovery engine for finding ideas like recipes, home and style inspiration, and more." (Pinterest)[217]

Pinterest launched native video in 2020 in the form of Pinterest video pins. Pinterest Video Pins have a cover image that captures your audience's attention. They play in users' feeds, so keep in mind that your audience may or may not have their audio on when they see your video. These video pins make Pinterest popular with retail and e-commerce brands because of videos that don't disappear with a feed, unlike other platforms, offering an excellent opportunity for evergreen marketing.

 Want to know more?

- Create Video Pins help.pinterest.com/en/business/article/video-pins

2.6   CREATE A VIDEO MARKETING PLAN

2.6.1   VIDEO MARKETING STRATEGIC PLAN AND ACTION PLAN

What's the difference between a strategy and a plan? A video marketing strategy is all about the destination and the path. Usually, a strategy doesn't change over the years.

A strategic plan is all about people, priorities, resources, and deadlines. Strategic plans can change.

Example of Video Marketing Strategic Plan

	NOW	NEXT	NEW	NOT
Assignment of time, resources, and budget	70%	20%	10%	0%
Market/target	Loyal customers	Customer segment with most growth potential	New market/ segment	Segment out of scope
Business Strategy	Keep doing it	Optimize for growth	Try out to learn	Stop doing or ignore
Video marketing tactics: examples	Create a series of native videos for YouTube and Facebook	Video ads with measurable business goals (not: "Get more video views") Repurpose older videos into social media formats to create engagement	Experiment with TikTok videos to learn about creating short, entertaining videos for a younger audience	Make corporate movies Create 30s TV ads and upload those to YouTube

Next step: create a video marketing action plan.

An action plan is a detailed plan outlining actions needed to reach one or more goals. Your video marketing action plan details who will do what and when, plus which budgets are available for video content creation and promotion. An example for the "Video Advertising" part could look a little like this:

	2022 Q1	2022 Q2	2022 Q3	2022 Q4
Creation of YouTube series of educational videos	Video production agency: 5 videos	Video production agency: 5 videos		
Promotion of YouTube video series		Advertising agency YouTube ads campaign 1		Advertising agency YouTube ads campaign 2
Creation of "behind the scenes – we're hiring" Facebook native video series	Advertising agency Facebook native video series: 3 videos			
Promotion of Facebook native video series	Advertising agency Facebook and Instagram video ads: 6 videos			
Budget	$80K	$80K		$10K

 It's always a good idea to put them in the form of a timeline or calendar. If it's in people's calendars, it gets done!

HERO, HUB, HELP AS A FRAMEWORK FOR YOUR CONTENT PUBLISHING CALENDAR

YouTube's Hero, Hub, Help framework is a rigorous way to tackle the daunting task of video marketing. The "triple h" approach provides a framework for planning, creating, and promoting content. Although it was initially developed for YouTube, you can apply it to any form of marketing.

 Use Google's Hero, Hub, Help model to plan your videos in the year.

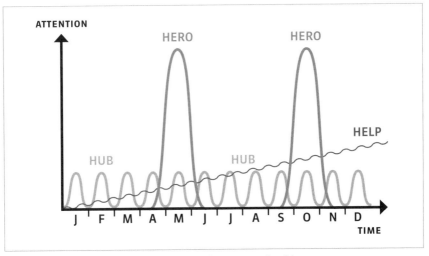

Hero-Hub-Help x=attention vs. y=months of the year

What are HERO moments?

According to Google, hero content is "big, tent-pole events that are designed to provide a massive step-change to your audience growth." Hero content is those big campaigns that build awareness of your brand and lead to lots of attention in a short amount of time.

Some examples:

- Video ad campaigns: large-scale, highly produced moments or events explicitly designed for brand awareness.
- Events, for example, webinars, keynote speeches, or presentations.

- Aftermovies and other event coverage bring the viewer into an experience (industry event, company outing, demonstration of product in action) and make them feel as though they're there. This is an opportunity to leverage 360 videos and VR for the ambitious.
- Original series: regularly scheduled "push content" targeted to your audience released at a regular cadence.

What are HUB moments?

HUB (or "always-on") content is regular, engaging content geared to an audience that already knows your brand, like your Instagram account or Facebook page's followers. The purpose of HUB content is to engage your audience and give them a reason to keep watching.

Brands are moving away from the old model of a few pieces of big content through the calendar, replacing it with an always-on model that reflects the thinking of a publisher and a more traditional advertiser. (Mowat, 2018)[218]

But how do you organize for this always-on model? Answer: by tapping into time-bound events, like the typical "Days of the Year." Examples are videos created on the occasion of Valentine's Day or Halloween.

HELP (or "evergreen") content is content people search for while in their consideration phase. With channels where search is the primary driver of new subscribers, evergreen content is more potent.

HELP content answers the questions that people are searching for. It appears in people's searches when they need to know something and drives both SEO and organic search ROI. (Mowat, 2018)[219]

UPLOAD SCHEDULE AND CONTENT COLLABORATION

As if using videos to create brand awareness is not enough, you're also obliged to post regularly and consistently. The moment you stop and take three or four months off, all your engagement on YouTube, TikTok, or Facebook will go down.

The next time you post something, the social media algorithms will not push the video the same way to your followers as they did before. Your reach is going to be significantly affected.

What is the ideal scheduling time? The best way is to learn this as you go:

Step 1: Whatever works for you and your schedule.

Step 2: Strive to have some sort of a schedule, e.g., Monday – Wednesday – Friday.

Step 3: Your audience will start with whoever is online at that time. Business audiences might prefer weekdays and business hours.

Step 4: Channel analytics for day and time with highest engagement rate and views.

Adopt an upload schedule, so your fans know when to tune in for new content. Consider communicating this in your channel trailer or reminding viewers of your videos. (YouTube Creator Academy)[220]

- For YouTube, twice a week is a nice sweet spot (on fixed hours/days, though).
- As long as you're following a schedule and keep it consistent for your audience, posting one to two times per month can still give you good results on Facebook.
- For TikTok, a schedule of semi-daily or at least multiple times a week is better.
- For Instagram, several times a week is essential.
- On Twitch, people tend to schedule streams in their calendar and get worried or frustrated when it doesn't happen.

 Batch record your videos on the same day. For example: record every Saturday morning, edit on Sunday, schedule out on weekdays.

Keep track of the posts and videos that get the most engagement on social and reschedule the posts every few months to re-invigorate your older videos.

If your video production is teamwork, use a literal calendar (Google Calendar or Outlook Calendar) to share not only your Hero, Hub, Help planning but also the content itself. Contrary to spreadsheet software like Excel, Calendars can:

- Have content moments recurring weekly, monthly, or yearly
- Have rich content in the Calendar Item, like Titles, Description, thumbnails, and other visual material (or links to Dropbox or WeTransfer for larger files).
- Manage user rights, like who can edit or view Calendar items
- Be shared and added to, e.g., the Calendars of your workhorse device (your laptop, not your smartphone).
- Be sent as an email to everyone involved in the project, for example, every Monday morning.

WHERE TO FIND INSPIRATION FOR YOUR VIDEO CONTENT PLAN

The Hero, Hub, Help framework helps, but gaps in your Content Calendar will still occur. One of the best ways to come up with content ideas is with a brainstorming session. Here are some content ideas to put you on the right track.

Content focus: food

- Create a new recipe with just five raw ingredients.
- Create a sandwich of epic proportions.
- Describe your most creative way to use leftovers.
- If a restaurant were to name something after you, what would it be? Describe it. (Bonus points if you give us a recipe!)
- Make a menu for a dinner party based on a favorite movie.
- Gordon Ramsay is coming over for dinner tonight. What do you serve to impress him?
- Share a healthy alternative to indulgent comfort food.
- What are the components of your ideal breakfast?
- What was your go-to "broke meal"?
- What's in your pantry?

Tech questions for an interview (with yourself or an expert in the field)

- Are there any tech gadgets you're eyeing? What gadget is at the top of your wish list?
- Are you a Mac or a PC user? iOS or Android?
- Describe a smartphone app you want to see on the market.
- Do you have a smartphone? Has it made your life easier or just different?
- How do you like to get your news or inspiration these days?
- How do you manage your online privacy? Are there certain things you won't post in certain places? Information you'll never share online? Or do you assume information about you is accessible anyway?
- How do you spend the majority of your online time? Which apps do you use daily?
- In what ways do you wish you were more tech-savvy?

- List five types of social media posts or messages you can't stand.
- Predict how our use of technology will change in the next five years.
- Name an outdated or obsolete technology you wish were still a part of modern life.
- Sometimes, we all need a break from these little glowing boxes. How do you know when it's time to unplug? What do you do to make it happen?
- What format did you start listening to music on?
- What's the longest you'd want to live without Internet access?
- Name a (board/video) game that you'll never get tired of.

Getting content ideas from your audience

You must be in the shoes of your audience if you want to create the best experience for them. (Schmittauer, 2017)[221]

Questions & Answers (Q&A) and Ask Me Anything (AMA) sessions are a great way to connect with your audience and start a dialogue. One way to begin with this type of video is to start with a list of FAQs that you often receive and make a video answering them. And from there, encourage your viewers to leave a comment on that video with more questions. This gives you a chance to follow up and create even more value for your audience.

Special holidays

 Out of inspiration for your videos? Use daysoftheyear.com for ideas!

The typical seasonal "Days of the" type topics are perfect for your Video Stories. Ask yourself (or your audience):

- What's your favorite month of the year? Why?
- Which holiday would you rather skip? Why?
- What is your favorite holiday? Why is it your favorite?
- Invent a holiday! Explain how and why everyone should celebrate.
- What major sporting event do you get most excited about?

JANUARY
- What are you looking forward to this year?
- What's going to be different this year?
- Is there a goal you'd like to accomplish by the end of this year?
- How's it going with your New Year's resolutions? Be honest!
- How was your year so far? Is your year off to a good start?

FEBRUARY
- How do you feel about Valentine's Day?
- Do you celebrate Valentine's Day? Why or why not?
- List the places you wouldn't mind being taken on Valentine's date.

MARCH
- Spring is coming – what Easter candy are you excited to see back on store shelves?
- What's on your spring to-do list?
- Have the past three months of your life been what you expected them to be?

APRIL
- Did you pull any pranks on April Fools' Day? Did you fall for any?
- What are the best (and worst) Fools' Day pranks you've seen online this year?
- Happy Earth Day! We think we're in charge of this planet just because we have smartphones. Which species do you think runs the show?
- Which movies deserve to win Oscars this year?

MAY
- Who is the mother figure in your life? Who are you a mother figure for?

JUNE
- Exactly half the year is now over. List things you want to do before the second half begins.
- What are you most proud of achieving so far this year?
- What's the most unexpected thing that's happened to you so far this year?
- What's on your "to-do" list this summer?
- What are you most looking forward to doing this summer?

JULY
- Have you started making any summer travel plans?

AUGUST
- How did/do you spend the dog days of summer?

SEPTEMBER
- Another school semester will soon begin. If you're in school, are you looking forward to starting classes? If you're out of school, what do you miss about it - or are you glad those days are over?

OCTOBER
- Describe your most memorable Halloween.
- Do you celebrate Halloween? Why or why not? Do you know how the Halloween tradition originated? Explain.
- What are the best Halloween costumes you've worn or seen?
- What is the best Halloween costume you have ever witnessed in person?

NOVEMBER
- It's the first week of November! What does this month make you think of?
- Happy Thanksgiving. What are you most thankful for this year?
- What are your favorite ways to stay warm in winter?
- What's on your winter reading list?

DECEMBER
- What are your most and least favorite things about the holiday season?
- What do you think you'll remember most from the last year?
- You're asked to nominate someone for TIME's Person of the Year. Who would it be, and why?
- Summarize your year with one sentence for each month.
- What's the single most important thing you accomplished this year?

Here's one of my personal favorites: International Day of Human Space Flight on 12 April. Some ideas:

- What's the most you'd pay for a ticket to visit space?
- If you could travel to any planet in our solar system, which world would you choose and why?
- If you were offered a free trip to Mars, would you go? Why or why not?
- Imagine NASA is building a new Voyager spacecraft, and like its earlier counterparts, it's going to carry the best of modern human culture inscribed onto a record. What belongs on there and why?

Get content ideas from interviewing someone interesting

Guest interviews and talk shows are centered around a flowing conversation with multiple participants. Ensure sharp sound quality for crisp dialogue, and consider minor post-production effects (i.e., name overlays and transitions). Having a guest adds to your credibility - especially if they are an expert in a field related to your product or service.

The Tonight Show Starring Jimmy Fallon

TWiT.tv provides news, commentary, help & how-to, reviews, and perspective on the latest trends in digital tech.

TwiT.tv host Leo Laporte takes calls from his podcast audience. Ask your audience (e.g., your Twitter followers) their opinion on the following tech-related topics. The answers will help you flesh out the content of a series of videos (podcast recordings) about technology.

What if... you could change the world?

- You have the power to enact a single law. What would it be?
- You're in charge today. You make the rules.
- If you had the attention of the entire world for two minutes, what would you say?
- If you had unlimited resources, what would you create?

What if... you would never fail? What if... you would never get caught?

- If you could do anything you wanted today, right this second, what would it be?
- If you could say anything to anyone without consequence, what would you say, and to whom?
- If there were no consequences, what's the evilest thing you would do?
- Tell us about something you would attempt if you were guaranteed not to fail (and tell us why you haven't tried it yet).

What if... you could go anywhere? Right now? For a long time? Forever?

- When teleportation is finally possible, where will you beam yourself first?
- If you could work from anywhere, where would you want to live, and why?
- If you were asked to spend a year living in a different location, where would you choose and why?
- If you could pause real life and spend some time living with a family anywhere in the world, where would you go?
- If you had the opportunity to live a nomadic life, traveling from place to place, would you do it? Do you need a home base? What makes a place "home" to you?
- What city would you retire to if money were no object?
- If you won two free plane tickets, where would you go?

What if... you could become something or someone entirely different? For a day? For the rest of your life?

- At full moon, you turn into a person who's the opposite of who you usually are. Describe this new you.
- Have you ever wondered what it would be like to be a member of the opposite sex for a day? What do you think life would be like?
- If you could become any type of animal, which would you choose to become? Would it be a winged animal? Why (not)?
- If you could become two people right now, what are the first two things you'd want to do?
- If you could wake up tomorrow as any other human being in the world, which person would you choose to be and why?
- If you were an inanimate object, what would you be and why? If you were a piece of furniture, what would you be?

From your (or an expert's) daily routine

- There's never enough time, is there? What would you do with an extra three hours today?
- Do you prefer sunrise or sunset? (Or is it all the same to you?). Are you a morning or night person? (Or are you "on" all day long?) Are you an early bird or a night owl?
- What's your favorite way to start the day?
- What's the first thing you do when you wake up in the morning? The last thing you do before going to sleep at night?
- Describe your perfect Saturday night.
- Describe your perfect Sunday morning.
- If you could clone yourself, how would you split up your responsibilities?
- Share three things you do every day without fail.
- Can you get work done while music is playing?
- When are you most productive?
- What's the first thing you do when you get off work/out of school?

From your (or a customer's) own home

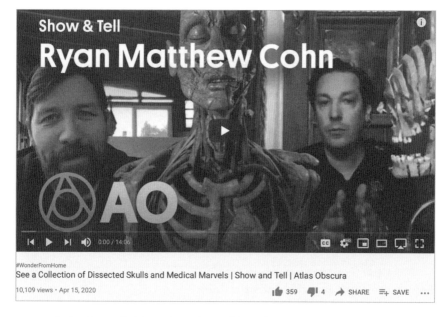

During the 2020 lockdown, alternative travel channel Atlas Obscura created the Show and Tell series. Founder Dylan used video call software to make virtual trips to Atlas Obscura friends with impressive unique collections in their own homes.

For e-commerce stores, from people's direct physical environment (their things):

- Describe which object you use for a purpose other than its intended one.
- Do you collect anything?
- Do you have a good luck charm?
- If you had to evacuate your home in an instant, what five items would you grab on your way out?
- Do you have a favorite work of art?
- You're moving into a smaller place. You have to get rid of almost everything, so what do you make sure you keep?
- What is your most treasured possession?
- Name a bizarre gift you received. Do you still have it?

From your (or an employee's) professional ambitions

Example for the finance/insurance industry (where you have to be careful not to appear to give financial advice).

- Describe a great boss you've worked with.
- Describe how you'd spend $1,000.
- Describe your ideal job - where would you work? What would you do?
- Has the economic climate affected you?
- How do you save money? What are you saving up for?
- If you could change one thing about your living situation, what would it be?
- What do you like most about your job? (Or studies, etc.)
- What does wealth mean to you?
- What would you do with a six-month break from work or school?
- What's worth paying top dollar for?
- What's the one luxury you can't live without?
- You're given a plot of land and have the financial resources to do what you please. What's the plan?

Every road trip is a story!

 Make a road trip and vlog about it. Ask your friends on Facebook or Instagram how they would plan it.

Perfect for car brands as road trip sponsors!

- Describe a scary stretch of road you've traveled.
- Describe the longest road trip you've ever taken.
- Describe your favorite place to drive.
- Discuss the best road trip you've ever taken.
- List your must-haves for a successful road trip.
- What would a road trip companion learn about you when traveling with you for the first time?
- What's your favorite part of visiting a new place? The food? The architecture? The people watching?

Creator collabs

Working with other creators is one of the most often cited ways to reach new viewers and boost your channel.

Collaboration, as it is most often referred to in the field of content creation, is when one brand/person/influencer and another brand/person/influencer come together to create. Creator A makes a video on his or her video channel and invites Creator B to be featured in the content. Often it will also happen the other way around in the same video creation session: Creator B will make a video of their presence and feature Creator A. (Schmittauer, 2017)[222]

Collabs are a great way to help get your content in front of established audiences who may be unfamiliar with your YouTube presence.

- Choose wisely: The most popular creator may not be the best choice; focus on audience reach and content style.
- Be social: It's called the creator community for a reason! The best collaborations are built out of genuine relationships formed through social interactions rather than business arrangements.
- Go beyond a one-off: Think about creating a repeatable format.

There are three main benefits of collaboration. (Cannell & Travis, 2018)

1   It exposes you to a new audience. The influencers you collaborate with have often already established an audience within a specific demographic or tribe of viewers.

2   It spreads out the work. When you collaborate, sometimes you cut the work of video creation in half and multiply the success.

3   It helps you learn. Pharrell Williams, musician, and entrepreneur, said, "Collaborate with people that you can learn from."

Make a goal of doing at least one collaboration per month or at least once every quarter.

RUN - SHOOT, UPLOAD, AND PROMOTE YOUR VIDEOS

There are three parts in a production: pre-production, production, and post-production.

3.1 PRE-PRODUCTION: PLANNING AND PREPARING

Pre-production is the process of planning some of the elements involved in a film, play, or other performance.

3.1.1 VIDEO PROJECT PLANNING

Questions to consider when creating a video (Deziel, 2020)[223]:

- Is special talent, software, or equipment needed to capture video content?
- Is special talent, software, or equipment needed to edit video content?
- How long does the video need to be to tell this story effectively? Would several smaller videos better serve the audience?
- Should the video be shot horizontally or vertically to fit its intended destination best?
- Have captions been added to ensure accessibility?

- Is the lighting sufficient to capture quality video in this environment? Would supplemental artificial lighting be helpful?
- Would on-screen text, charts, or other graphics add to this video?
- Would background music or sound effects add to this video? Are additional rights needed to use such audio?
- Which platform should this video be posted or hosted on?
- Which keywords should be used in the video title, description, and tags to optimize this video's discoverability through search?

Tips for video project managers (Clarke, 2019)[224]:

- Rehearse: Get everyone together for a short practice to save time in production.
- Leave time for reshoots: Overestimate the time needed for travel, shooting, and editing by 20%, so you aren't rushed.
- Make a list: Write a checklist for the people and gear you'll need on the day of the shoot. Note which items use batteries or need to be charged ahead of time.
- Schedule shoots well in advance: If you're using employees as actors, give them ample heads up so their plans don't cause delays.
- Let it be collaborative: As much as you try to plan for everything, leave creative wiggle room for others to have ideas. Actors may find a better way to say a line, or you may find a shot looks better with the actors standing rather than seated.
- Focus on solving people's problems to get past on-camera nervousness.

3.1.2 **VIDEO PLAN**

Decide on the overall structure of your videos. Each video plan has a few essential elements: the length of the video, the intro, the outro, how your video starts, whether it has subtitles, etc.

 Don't worry too much about things that don't seem to work. If you start being too critical too soon in the process, you'll create your roadblocks.

What helps is the skill of editing in your head. This takes practice because you might not always know what to do next. If you're just getting started, record a little bit extra, see what works, and learn how to start editing in your head as you go.

Also: plan for B-roll. B-roll, B roll, B-reel, or B reel are supplemental or alternative footage intercut with the main shot in film and television production. This can be footage of the surroundings of your video location or a time-lapse of you preparing for the shoot. Record this with your camera phone on a tripod and just let it roll (you don't need the audio).

An excellent shooting tip is to move around and get different angles and locations. Use the space, change up the rooms throughout your video, and it will keep people much more engaged.

3.1.3   VIDEO OUTLINE

A video outline contains the major story points of the video written in short paragraphs or bullet points with no dialogue and minimal description. This provides the structure and action of the film with little detail. (Ascher & Pincus, 2020)[225]

Write an outline with a numbered or bulleted list plus the keyword phrases and essential names.

Learn the key points and talk naturally to the camera. Aim for creating conversational videos – similar to those by British YouTuber Tom Scott.

YouTubers have to declare ads. Why doesn't anyone else?

3,590,749 views • Feb 15, 2021   👍 244K   👎 2.2K   ➤ SHARE   ≡₊ SAVE   ...

Tom Scott

- Have a plan and talking points. Make sure you hit all the points you want to make.
- You can wing certain videos like tutorials, but only if you have a thorough understanding of the main concepts.

Having an outline at hand helps you cut out filler content and lulls. No matter how good you are at winging it, an outline will save you lots of recording and editing time.

Scripted videos tend to perform better. Why? They give viewers a lot more value in a short amount of time. The fact that it brought them value is what they will remember and why they will stick with you long-term.

That said, don't read word for word from a script. The more you look at the script, the less you connect to your viewers.

 If you script only one thing, script the intro. Never wing your introduction.

3.2 PRODUCTION: FILM SCHOOL BASICS

Crew Size. Finding the right crew size is a delicate balancing act.

An OPC (One-Person Crew) saves significantly on the cost of labor. If the crew is too small for the job's complexity, crew members get overburdened, and the work is inefficient and slow.

The larger the crew involved, the more support (cars, meals, accommodation) these people need, which requires even more people.

The larger the crew, the more expensive each hour of work becomes, which adds pressure to the shoot and makes it much harder to experiment and try out ideas. (Ascher & Pincus, 2020)[226]

 Start as a One-Person Crew. This will be harder, but you'll learn a broader range of skills. As soon as the budget allows you to include more contractors, you'll be able to brief them better because, at some point in time, you've done it yourself.

- Has the business side of running your channel become too time-consuming for you? If business functions prevent you from creating videos the way you want, think about what can be done to bring on more people so that you can focus more of your time on creative aspects.
- Are there processes or issues that are limiting you from further growth? Consider your current work processes and challenges, plus what would happen as your business expands. There may be off-the-shelf solutions to help you overcome some of these limitations.
- Do you have the next steps you want to take, but need support to reach your goals? Your goals may be to increase your channel reach, negotiate a brand deal, or launch your merchandise. Try prioritizing your next steps and looking for help in those areas first.

 Learn about building your team and other business skills at YouTube Creator Academy[227].

Most creators start off working alone, and if their channel turns into a business venture, they look to building a team to help take it to the next level. There are different types of positions that can help you scale your business. Figuring out who to hire first will depend on your budget, skills, and priorities. Here are the main categories:

- **Content production**. Many creators enjoy being hands-on with their production. But it's not always feasible to handle everything alone. Based on the scope and volume of your shoots, you may want to seek out creative talents such as a writer, producer, director, crew, sound engineer, or editor.
- **Business / Legal**. There are specific roles that may be appropriate to fill here, especially if you don't have expertise in these areas.
    - A **business manager** manages the day-to-day business. Your business manager would generally be responsible for overseeing the business activities and staff. He or she would take care of payroll, banking, and other logistics.
    - An **accountant** would focus on bookkeeping and taxes. Your business manager may also do the bookkeeping. In contrast, accountants typically have a certification that qualifies them to do tasks such as conducting an audit or representing you before a tax authority.
    - A **lawyer** can help negotiate and review contracts as well as advise on legal matters such as copyright. Although lawyers often charge by the hour, some choose to work on commission. Laws vary geographically, so try looking for a lawyer who is licensed in your locale.
- **Representation**. Some creators choose to have formal representation. A manager can provide counsel, advice, and general career direction. Your manager is invested in you for the long term, so it's an ongoing business relationship. An agent is someone you would hire for more transactional, short-term business opportunities (such as pitching an endorsement). Agents typically specialize so that you may use more than one along the way.

3.2.1   BEHIND THE CAMERA

Recording in progress? Do not disturb! To create a distraction and noise-free setup:

- Turn off the fan and air conditioner.
- Turn off or mute email and messaging alerts from your phone and computer.
- Remove items from your background that distract viewers from your brand and messaging.
- Add neutral wall art or plants to make the backdrop look aesthetically pleasing.

Tripod. Keep your camera as steady as possible. Use a tripod whenever you can. Mount the camera at eye level (not in your trembling hands and not right under your nose). Keep a distance of a maximum of 1m from the lens.

Rule of thirds. Keep the central subject out of the middle of your shot. Instead, put the subject off to the side, with an interesting background filling in the rest of the shot. This will make the video look dynamic and interesting. (Even if the person talking isn't.) (Clarke, 2019)[228]

Mind your composition when you self-shoot a video. Don't fill up the entire frame with your face. Keep it at a distance of about 1m from the camera lens. The perfect framing would be from your chest to slightly above your head. Ensure that the camera is at your eye level – not too low or too high. Ideally, position yourself in the center of the frame to maintain symmetry but leave enough headroom.

Headroom is that space between a person's head and the top of the frame.

In a close-up or medium close-up, you can place the subject's eyes about a third of the screen height from the top. So the focus of attention is about a third of the way from the top and one of the sides. That said, centered framing has its place too. (Ascher & Pincus, 2020)[229]

Backgrounds. Be particularly attentive to what's directly behind the subject, such as plants that may seem to be growing out of a person's head or activity that distracts from what you want the audience to focus on. (Ascher & Pincus, 2020)[230]

 Aim to use a backdrop that fits your client. If you're selling to large enterprises, your background will show large airy offices or cityscapes. If you're selling to startups, brick walls or open office floors. (Wistia)[231]

High and low angles. With many people, it just looks unflattering to see the underside of their chin or nose. Filming a high-angle shot from somewhat above the subject may add an interesting flavor, or sometimes it may seem to diminish the person. (Ascher & Pincus, 2020)[232]

 The best way to avoid video weight gain is to have the camera lens slightly higher than your eye level and tilt the camera down. This slims your face and pretty much everything else. (Schmittauer, 2017)[233]

3.2.2   LIGHTING

Lighting allows you to define what is hidden and what is revealed within each shot. (Wistia)[234]

Examine each source for these factors: What kind of shadow does it cast (crisp or diffuse)? Where (what angle) is it coming from? How bright is it relative to other lights (the lighting contrast)? What color is it? (Ascher & Pincus, 2020)[235]

The sun is a giant key light. Position the subject relative to the sun as you would using a key light. Make sure the sun isn't shining directly into a subject's eyes.

 At noon, the sun can shine too brightly to use for lighting your shots. Schedule your recording sessions in the morning or late afternoon (the so-called Golden Hours) when the sun is low on the horizon and has a warm cast. Noon is the absolute worst time to film.

If you use natural lighting in an indoor setting, make sure you face a window every time you take a video. Ensure the window is not behind you because the light reflection into the camera will almost certainly guarantee poor video quality. (Olson, 2020)[236]

The Blair Witch Project is a 1999 American supernatural horror film that features found footage from a group of friends who get lost in the woods.

Lighting setups to avoid:

- Light (e.g. a window with natural light) behind the subject. This will create a dark silhouette.
- Overhead light. This will create unflattering shadows under your eyes and nose.
- Never use your smartphone's flashlight (except if you're going for the Blair Witch Project look).

Recording indoors gives you more control over your lighting conditions. To avoid distracting shadows:

- keep your subjects away from walls,
- place them against dark rather than light walls,
- position furniture or props to break up the shadows,
- use diffusion to soften secondary lights.

 Position lights above a subject's eye level, tilted down at a 30 to 45° angle. If your angle is too high, it will cause a nose shadow on your subject's lips. (Ascher & Pincus, 2020)[237]

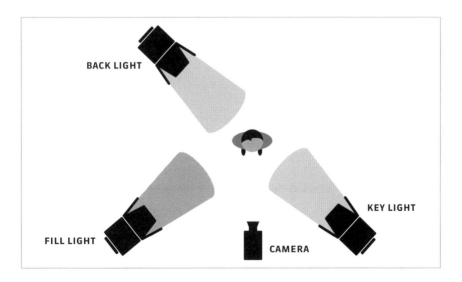

3 Point Lighting

The standard three-point lighting is easy to set up and allows you to control shadows.

1   **Key light**: The leading light (slanted) at the front. Place it 30 to 45° to the side of the subject. Popular TikTok content creators use ring lights to provide additional lighting for their videos. Ring light significantly improves the quality of the video and is very affordable. (Olson, 2020)[238]

2   **Backlight or hair light**: Lights the subject from behind to pull the object/person away from the background and remove shadows. You can leave out this light when the subject already stands out from the environment.

3   **Fill light**: To fill in any remaining shadows. Place the light 30-45° to the subject's side, on the opposite side of the key light. Fill lights often have so-called "barn doors," so you can attach light diffusers (filters, softboxes, or umbrellas). You can leave this light out in areas that are already well-lit or to create dramatic shadows.

The hard part is keeping the bright lights out of the frame; you want to see the light, not "the lights."

3.2.3 **HOW TO LOOK GOOD ON CAMERA**

How you act on camera doesn't have to be the same as you are all the time. That is not weird at all: you naturally act differently when you're with your kids, boss, or audience. The camera is just another "person" you're talking to.

Two things when you're talking in front of a camera: be authentic and fun. People can detect if you're doing it for the money or trying to copy other people. (Olson, 2020)[239]

 Don't appear flawless. Show a charming flaw. Confidence attracts, but vulnerability endears. (Sivers, 2020)[240]

How to dress for the camera (Clarke, 2019)[241]:

- Dress to connect with your audience and match your message. If you want to convey reliability to a prominent New York financial services firm, wear formal business attire. If you're trying to connect with a small startup, a hoodie might be more appropriate.
- Wear solid colors - complicated patterns often look funny on film. Stick to black or mid-range colors like blue or green. Avoid striped or white shirts: they take the attention away from the eyes.
- Don't wear sunglasses: people want to see your eyes.
- No hats. (They distract from the face.)

The power of makeup by Nikkie Tutorials

Look clean and presentable out of respect for your audience. Make it part of your "getting ready for recording" routine to making yourself presentable:

- comb your hair
- use makeup in the right skin tone to remove the shine and hide details that might distract
- tuck your shirt in or straighten your tie
- do a quick scoop and swoop if your bra tends to get uncomfortable
- pull up your socks.

You don't have to say "Showtime!" All I can tell you is that it works for me.

Just remember, video works best when the person on camera is having a conversation with one person. (Clarke, 2019)[242] Always, always, always look at the lens of the camera. (Schmittauer, 2017)[243] When you shoot a video for a virtual event, ensure that speakers look directly into the camera and adopt a friendly and open approach. (Meerman Scott & Manafy, 2020)[244]

Practice makes perfect or at least makes you confident. Get used to seeing yourself on camera by recording yourself for at least one minute every day. Maintain eye contact with the camera to build a connection with your viewers.

Stand up if you can. A straight posture helps you breathe more easily. Don't talk with your arms folded in front of your body. Don't scratch, fidget, or fiddle with a pen, as it can distract your audience.

To project positivity, use open hand gestures. Doing this will show that you want to share something interesting with your audience. Don't go overboard with the motions, as overexpression could distract.

Always start and end with a smile. Don't start talking immediately. Give yourself some space first. Breathe in, breathe out.

 Do you keep looking at yourself while filming? Put a Post-it Note over your screen so that you can focus on the lens! (Trip, 2020)[245]

Speak lower, slower, and with certainty: it conveys authority. Speak in a clear and frank voice but vary the tone and pace. Move your hands some, but not so much that it's distracting. Take pauses after sentences. It'll help you remember to slow down, but it also creates suspense. The more knowledgeable and passionate you are about the subject, the more confident you'll feel talking about it on camera. Beyond that, practice is essential. (Cannell & Travis, 2018)[246]

Your fans are your friends. Speak to them like real people. Be weird. Prove you're a natural person. (Sivers, 2020)[247]

You can write lines on cue cards. A low-budget technique is to cut a hole in the center of the cue card for the lens. A better solution is to use a **teleprompter**, which mounts in front of the lens and displays written copy from a tablet, smartphone, or computer. (Ascher & Pincus, 2020)[248]

Use a large clamp (e.g., the Goos-e Pro XL) to repurpose your iPad as a teleprompter. Use teleprompter for iPad or the native Pages app in presenter mode. Before pressing "record," swipe slowly upwards from the bottom of the screen to reveal the dock, then tap and drag the teleprompter icon from the dock onto the screen to use the teleprompter and camera app at the same time.

Another possibility is to use a hardware teleprompter mirror that sits on your smartphone (e.g., the Podcaster Parrot). If you have an iPhone, you have the added benefit of using your Apple Watch as a viewfinder and remote for the video recording function.

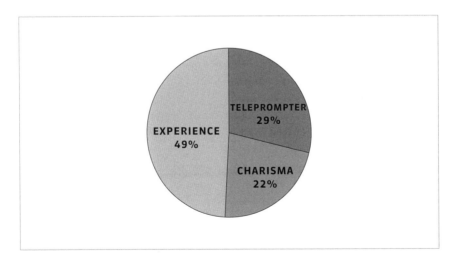

How I manage to talk with ease and confidence on camera.

THE BEST GEAR FOR SOLO VIDEO

If you're a video producer or marketer, you know how hard it can be to make a video by yourself. You might be asking yourself, "How do I set up my camera? How do I make sure the shot's in focus? How do I not sound flat on camera?"

These are all tricky questions that can stop you from creating your next piece of content. You have the idea, but you just need to know how to do it yourself in the best way possible. (Wistia)[249]

 Pick gear that is easy to transport in your handbag or backpack and whip it out fast when inspiration strikes.

WEBCAM CAMERA ON DESKTOP, LAPTOP, OR TABLET

A webcam is a video camera that feeds or streams an image or video in real-time to or through a computer to a computer network, such as the Internet. The image sensor of webcams is much smaller, usually resulting in lower quality video.

Most webcams also don't include a high-quality microphone, which means that the sound you get on a webcam video is often of lower quality than you might want. You can compensate by sitting as close to the webcam as possible and speaking loudly and clearly. (Miller, 2008)[250]

 Use Zoom to record from your computer or tablet. Organize a meeting with you as the only attendee. If you're self-conscious about the way you look, you can even use Zoom's "touch up appearance" feature.

If you're using an external video source, you can't just plug the video feed directly into your computer. Use HDMI video converter dongles like Elgato Cam Link to shoot video through the USB port to a PC or Mac.

SMARTPHONE CAMERA

Your smartphone (or tablet) is the perfect starter kit for video production because you already have it.

These days, you can shoot, edit, and upload YouTube videos with the average smartphone, as long as you have an Internet connection. Forget the fancy equipment and expensive gear. (Cannell & Travis, 2018)[251]

Some of the more recent iPhones and Samsungs – among others – have made tremendous upgrades in the camera hardware and software department, making it possible to take 4K high definition (HD) videos. (Olson, 2020)[252]

 When filming with your phone, always use the camera on the back (not the front-facing camera above the screen) - it's more powerful and will provide a cleaner image.

DIGITAL CAMERAS

Feel more confident shooting video? Then get off the smartphone and give your videos that professional look with a digital camera.

DSLRs and mirrorless cameras are made by companies like Canon, Sony, and Nikon. Mirrorless cameras are very similar to DSLRs - except a lot smaller. Canon appears to be the most popular brand for vloggers who can afford it.

The Canon EOS 70D, together with the Joby GorillaPod "bendy" tripod and an external microphone, was the main ingredient of the famous "Casey Neistat vlog setup." Other vloggers prefer Canon's M50, the R-series or Powershot mirrorless cameras, while the Sony ZV-1 also gets good reviews.

 With most DSLR or mirrorless cameras, recording switches off after 20 or 30 minutes. This can be very annoying!

Don't pin yourself to specific camera brands or types. Camera hardware gets better and better all the time. Even professional video producers might not have the same camera for very long. It doesn't matter how high-end your camera gear is; if you don't know how to use it, you'll still make bad videos.

The criteria tech YouTuber Marques Brownlee looks for in a camera are: (Brownlee, 2021)[253]

- high quality
- easy to shoot
- easy to use
- long battery life.

Potential extra features can make your life as a video producer easier. Some examples:

- Face detection autofocus: the tech that allows the camera to focus on your face while you move closer and farther away
- Lenses that offer wide-angle zooms
- More creative control when it comes to lighting and exposure.

On the downside:

- DSLR cameras are much heavier and bulkier than smartphones.
- The equipment takes time to set up.

Put your video device on a tripod whenever you can. And if you need to go "handheld," use a nearby wall or chair to steady yourself. And if you have to "move-in" to shoot something close up, physically move the camera in. (Not the zoom.) (Clarke, 2019)[254]

A gimbal (for example, the Ronin-S Gimbal) is a pivoted support that permits the rotation of an object about an axis. Gimbals can take a while to calibrate correctly but are perfect with action cameras like the GoPro.

EXTERNAL MICROPHONES

The magic of editing can make up for a lack in personality or original content, but NOT for lousy audio. Bad audio can ruin even the best video footage. Your viewers will forgive many things, but they will not forgive audio that they cannot understand. To create the best experience for your audience, you'll want to make sure you have the right microphone for the job.

When the sound of your voice bounces off the walls of the room, this creates an echo or makes your voice sound hollow. How to fix this:

- Buy soundproofing material (like acoustic foam panels),
- Hang heavy studio curtains, or
- Throw some thick yoga mats, blankets, or cushions on the floor.

Hold the microphone as close to the audio source as possible. Try to get it as close to the subject's mouth as possible.

Internal microphones pick up audio of the environment, so try to work with external microphones whenever possible. Use a dynamic or podcast microphone for recordings onto your PC. Some suggestions for USB microphones include: Audio Technica's AT2020USB+, Razer's Seiren Elite (popular with gamers), Elgato's Wave 3, and Rode's NT-USB Mini.

To avoid popping sounds, add a pop filter or talk slightly over the microphone. While recording, avoid bumping the mic or what it's attached to.

A lavalier microphone or lavalier is a small clip-on microphone that allows for hands-free operation. It doesn't pick up any other sounds, except if you accidentally touch it with your hands.

Lavaliers are pretty unobtrusive and are easy to use when there isn't a sound recordist. (Ascher & Pincus, 2020)[255] RODE lavaliers offer good audio quality at a reasonably low price.

For vlogging, use a lightweight shotgun microphone (like a RODE Shotgun Microphone) as an external microphone you can attach to your camera. To avoid the sound of wind blowing, pull a windscreen over your microphone. This so-called deadcat cover blocks air from moving across the mic.

If you don't want to record the audio onto your camera, use the H1N Zoom Recorder with a lavalier microphone plugged in. To be extra safe, record audio with the on-device microphone as well.

 When you're caught outside without a good windscreen, use your body, the flap of your coat, or a building to shelter the mic from the wind. Hide a lavalier under clothing or put the tip of a wool glove over it. (Ascher & Pincus, 2020)[256]

ACTION CAMERAS AND DRONES

GoPro manufactures action cameras that are small, rugged, water-resistant, and highly automated. A GoPro can be mounted on a helmet, on a bike, or inside or outside a car and comes with its mobile apps and video-editing software. GoPro is perfect for wide-angle shots, for example, for extreme sports or other outdoor activities. This makes it a great second camera (audio is not so great on a GoPro).

Drones (like DJI drones) are flying robots that can be equipped with a remote-controlled camera. Since you would only hear the propellers or the wind, drone footage usually comes without audio.

An affordable drone can do overhead shots that once required a helicopter or plane, as well as lower-height tracking shots (like following a car through a forest or a jogger through a park) that would be impossible with an aircraft. (Ascher & Pincus, 2020)[257]

➕ Want to know more?

- If you buy only one video book, make it this one: *The Filmmaker's Handbook: A Comprehensive Guide for the Digital Age: Fifth Edition*, by Steven Ascher & Edward Pincus.
- Watch FREE filmmaking videos ranging from screenwriting to editing and advance your skills from beginner to expert as soon as possible at moviola. com.
- Vimeo Video School: Make better videos with tips from the Vimeo team, industry leaders, and friendly faces from the community. vimeo.com/blog/category/video-school.
- Wistia's (excellent) Guide to Video Marketing. Learn practical tips on how to elevate your video marketing efforts. wistia.com/about/video-marketing-guide
- Consult video production tutorials on YouTube channels by companies like Shutterstock, Aputure, and StudioBinder or follow video experts like Peter McKinnon, Tom Buck, Tom Antos, Potato Jet (Gene Nagata), Parker Walbeck, Gerald Undone, DSLR Video Shooter (Caleb Pike), Film Riot (the Conolly brothers), and DIY Perks (Matt Perks).

3.3 POST-PRODUCTION

Post-production includes all stages of video production occurring after shooting or recording individual video fragments.

When it comes to editing, the general rule of thumb is that you want to make it as long as it needs to be but as short as possible.

Assume that you will spend most time editing your videos (compared to shooting them). On average, most YouTube creators say they have a runtime of four to six hours of research, recording, and editing per video. So the sooner you come up with a workflow that makes your life easier, the better.

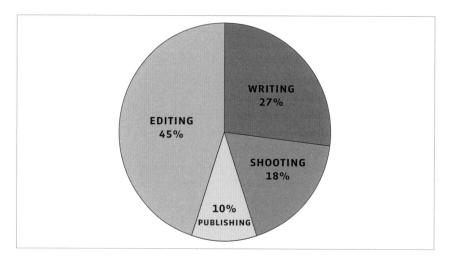

Designer Matt Birchler (Birchtree.me) broke down his time management for the produc-tion of three videos.[258]

3.3.1 EDITING BASICS

 The best way to make your video shorter is to aim for short when you start. The second best way is to internalize another old showbiz adage: When in doubt, cut it out. (Stockman, 2011)[259]

The goal of editing is to keep engagement level and eye attention high without becoming exhausting. Go easy on special effects, animation effects, and transitions between clips.

Avoid these four mistakes that frequently cause people to stop viewing videos:

- Poor sound quality or over-reliant on sound
- No personal/emotional connection
- Blurry or shaky picture quality
- Too slow to get to the point

The following basic editing features may improve your video:

- Add subtitles whenever possible. Use Rev.com, Limecraft (a Belgian startup!) or Kapwing.
- There are numerous editing and compositing apps to remove unwanted camera shake, including Adobe After Effects and Premiere Pro, DaVinci Resolve, Apple Final Cut Pro X, and Avid Media Composer. Some are astonishingly sophisticated and can make a bouncy, handheld shot look dolly smooth. (Ascher & Pincus, 2020)[260]
- If you want to hide your edits (e.g., where you cut out your "um"s) or for comedic effect, you can crop in on your face. Another thing you can do to hide your cuts is to insert B-roll footage or stock video.
- If your audio sounds off, you can smooth out or adjust the audio levels.
- Adding some sound effects to your videos for transitions, or when stuff pops up on the screen, or when a text comes on the screen helps keep the viewers engaged, helping them watch longer.
- Add Other People's Content. But be careful: Clipping other people's content is a bit black hat.

 Use software like Camtasia or Movavi for screen recordings or learn how to activate screen recording on your iPad or iPhone. Don't record audio and keep the clips short to avoid copyright claims.

In video production, the footage is raw, unedited material as originally filmed by a movie camera or recorded by a video camera, which typically must be edited to create a motion picture, video clip, television show, or similar completed work.

Once you've put in the voice-over, interview quotes, or vlog bits, you also know which fill shots or B-roll would match what quote. For example, when a vlogger talks about a fire truck, you put an image of a fire truck over or after the section. (Trip, 2020)[261] Stock video can be helpful to save time. But choosing stock footage relevant to your video is most important. Random clips make the video "not personal." (Wistia)[262]

Intro clip: You can have someone create a quick logo reveal video with or without sound or images of you. This would play before the video or before you deliver the content. (Wistia)[263]

Lower thirds: Usually includes your name, social media handles, website, and video title. They can also be CTAs throughout the video (to go to another video, website, blog, article, …). (Wistia)[264]

On-screen graphics: Pictures or words to illustrate the points you make in your video. Do not overdo graphics, especially if they're not custom-made to fit the branding. Cfr, animations in PowerPoint. Keep a good structure in key points, titles … (Wistia)[265]

An editing template (confusingly called Project in iMovie) is a standardization of the design of your video. Think about the following (Trip, 2020)[266]:

- Bumper for the series: a few seconds of video for branding and recognizability
- Sound logo: your company logo, perhaps animated, with sound or music
- Lower thirds: text bar at the bottom of the screen in the style of the company
- Titles: full-screen or split-screen title screen(s)
- Transparent logo at the top or bottom of the screen
- End screen with logo / call to action.

Music track: Music is a powerful force in videos. Music and how it defines pacing throughout the video can significantly impact the audience's emotions and energy.

3.3.2 EDITING HARDWARE AND SOFTWARE

Most digital cameras have one or more slots for inserting a flash memory card. Memory cards are small (some are tiny), and you can carry them in a case that fits in your pocket. When you remove a memory card from the camera, the first thing is to back up the files by copying them to external drives for safekeeping. Then the camera card can be erased and reused. (Ascher & Pincus, 2020)[267]

These camera cards are often SanDisk memory cards. If you want a portable external harddrive to back up larger video files, consider LaCie Rugged External Hard Drives or Samsung Portable SSD T5 or T7.

Get cloud storage ready. You don't want all these video files sitting on your phone, especially if it's the phone you use regularly. Create a Dropbox, Box, or Google Drive account, and download their apps to your phone so that you can quickly and easily upload your video footage. You can also opt to upload the video files to YouTube directly in private and download the MP4 from the back end for further editing. Free storage! (Schmittauer, 2017)[268]Invest in a Synology NAS with 10 Gbit connection if you want to literally do it like the pros.

A classic editing rig usually involves a powerful desktop computer and one (or more) large, high-resolution screens. A creative industry favorite since its debut in 1998 has always been the Apple iMac family. Lately, other Apple products like the MacBook Pro laptop or even the iPad Pro are powerful enough to edit videos.

On the PC side, Microsoft Surface Studio gets honorable mentions, the heavy-duty Dell G-series, and the Acer Predator Orion 9000.

Some basic editing software is free or comes with reasonably affordable price plans. Features are limited, but they're perfect for beginners. A few examples:

- iMovie is a free video-editing software exclusively for Mac and iOS users. Its easy-to-use interface makes it a favorite for many on-the-go users.
- DaVinci Resolve is a free color correction and non-linear video editing application for macOS, Windows, and Linux.
- YouTube's built-in YouTube editor packs in some simple but powerful functionality. You can easily trim, splice, or cut your existing videos after upload - or even perform simple edits entirely within your browser. Use

it for censoring (blurring out) the faces of people who didn't give their permission to be featured in your video.

- WeVideo: Unlike iMovie, WeVideo supports different platforms like Mac, Windows, mobile, and the web.
- Wave.video is an online video maker you can use to create powerful and engaging videos for your audience.
- Quik was initially built for GoPro users as an on-the-go editing tool, but you can also use it to edit videos and images captured on other devices.
- LumaFusion provides desktop-grade video editing on an iPad – and even on iPhone. The app scythes through 4K footage while freeing you from the limitations of simpler fare. You get a half-dozen video tracks, six additional audio tracks, a slew of transitions, incredible layer effects, and audio filters.
- Adobe Premiere Rush is a video editing app that uses AI. The tool gives users two types of editing. The first, freeform mode, gives you the flexibility to control all aspects of the editing process. Automatic, the second option, creates your video using smooth transitions once you've added all elements.
- Adobe Premiere Pro is a timeline-based video editing software application developed by Adobe Systems and published as part of the Adobe Creative Cloud licensing program.
- Final Cut Pro is a series of non-linear video editing software programs that allow you to edit and synchronize audio and video from multiple sources (cameras + microphones). Final Cut Pro uses layers to add media by dragging and dropping.

3.4 DISTRIBUTION & PROMOTION

Once it's all complete, please select the highest possible quality level your video platform allows, export your whole video project as an MP3, MP4, WMV, or MOV file, and it's ready for marketing!

Depending on the platform, uploading the video is just the start. Add metadata - descriptive details that can help people find your video - before you click Publish. Metadata contributes to discovery, so make sure you use words and images that provide an accurate and compelling glimpse of what viewers can expect.

The bare minimum is to upload your video natively to Facebook, LinkedIn, and YouTube. Create Once, Publish Everywhere (COPE) is an established strategy for (video) content creation and distribution. Although this seems like the most time and cost-efficient way to publish your videos, you should not interpret it literally.

A more nuanced version of the COPE strategy is GaryVee's Content Model[269], developed by Internet personality Gary Vaynerchuk. The underlying idea is to repurpose your videos to create bonus content:

- Use just the audio to create podcasts.
- Tools like Anchor.FM or Buzzsprout will distribute your podcast for you (Spotify, Apple Podcasts, iTunes, Stitcher, etc.).
- Use just the visuals without the audio to repurpose further under a new video or pitch.
- Use Ezgif.com to create a GIF from your video and add that to your email message. Add a play button overlay to your GIF to encourage subscribers to click through to your video.
- Transcribe it and turn it into an article, thus helping your SEO, too.
- One of the best features of YouTube is its automatic transcript capability. People can add and view transcripts, also called closed captions, for videos. Rev.com and Otter.ai offer machine-generated transcription services.
- Take out tweetable bits and post them on Twitter.
- Post short video clips on Facebook, Instagram, or LinkedIn.
- Add subtitles and make short episodes out of the video.

The workflow for GaryVee's Content Model doesn't end there.

After this initial round of content publishing, take the time to respond to comments. Use these comments and questions to create a second round of content, for example, by including user-generated content from your audience in your newsletter. This will incentivize other viewers to come up with "good" questions or comments.

 At the end of the video, say that you stay online about one hour after uploading to respond to comments.

Chiming in with your viewers in the comments has a massive payoff. First, you're going to get more views and comments from your audience because the amount of interaction shows YouTube that it is an engaging video worth spreading to a larger audience. But even better, you're showing your audience that you don't just drop the mic when you share your ideas in a video. You're going to continue to talk with them and exchange ideas. (Schmittauer, 2017)[270]

Interacting with your audience paves the way for organic video promotion. But what if you've just started? How can you promote your video home?

The obvious choice is to include it in your owned media by:

- Embedding videos on your web pages
- Driving traffic to your videos by mentioning them in your newsletters.

3.4.1 PROMOTING YOUR CHANNEL

In a social network, you are essentially subscribing to individuals who are sharing content. (Brennan, 2020)[271]

Subscribers are viewers who've indicated they want to see more of your content and click the Subscribe button on your channel. Subscribers are critical to your success on YouTube because they tend to spend more time watching your channel than viewers who aren't subscribed - and if they have notifications turned on, they'll be alerted when you post something new. They can also view your newly published videos in their Subscriptions feed. (YouTube Creator Academy)[272]

YouTube Channel subscriber numbers are mostly vanity metrics! Except if they turn on notifications, they don't even get alerted when you've uploaded a new video. What counts is the quality (not the quantity) of your channel subscribers and of the videos you've uploaded.

Promote your channel via your owned media:

- Include the URL of your video channel in your email signature
- Link to your channel in your Linktree or in the bio space of other social media platforms that allow for it.

 [YT channel link]?sub_confirmation=1 (this will prompt YT channel subscribe pop-up)

You may have heard of "sub for subs," but asking viewers of someone else's videos, for example, to subscribe to your channel with the promise of returning the favor will only make you look desperate. Also, don't buy subscribers, followers, or views because these will only bring you fake audiences. You can get demonetized for these inactive audiences even years later.

The Comment Method

1   Subscribe to +/- 10 relevant channels (more will just stress you out) with a similar topic, size (amount of subscribers), and audience

2   Hit the bell so you get notified.

3   Comment very quickly to rank your comment + get noticed by others while watching the same video. They might click on your profile pic, see your channel, then subscribe/like/comment, etc.

The Comment Method is frowned upon when it's too obvious, so make sure to post something thoughtful. Fight the urge to link to your channel or videos.

Don't get too stuck on the lack of likes and comments on your videos. It's true: likes are good for social proof, and they pad your ego. The Comment Method can help you in the beginning but only do it until you've reached your point of diminishing returns. This depends on where you are in your journey. Tip: do it until you get to 1,000 subs, then only do it casually. Focus on optimizing your video marketing instead: this will result in a much higher ROI.

3.4.2 VIDEO DISTRIBUTION AND PROMOTION

Never promote something until people can take action, or you might waste the one moment you had their attention. Are your fans telling their friends? If not, then don't waste time promoting it yet. Keep working, improving, and creating, until your fans are telling their friends about you. (Sivers, 2020)[273]

However, what you can do is be smart about how and where you distribute your video. Content is 20% creation and 80% distribution!

Distribution is the vital last step in the video marketing process. No matter how awesome your video is, people won't just bump into it. You need to promote it to the right audience proactively. Apart from knowing which platforms your audience prefers to consume your video content on, you also need to understand how to promote your videos to them. Here are a few pointers to get you started (Kane, 2020)[274]:

- Email it to your customer or subscriber base. Your email subscribers are one of your most significant assets. Not only because they buy from you, but because they're your unpaid PR team.
- Use short, 30 second to one-minute teasers optimized for Facebook, Instagram & Twitter to cross-promote longer videos on YouTube. Use both sponsored and organic posts to give your video as much traction as possible.
- Another great place to promote your video content is on forums and online communities.

 Don't just drop links all over the place, e.g., Facebook groups or subreddits. This will get you blocked because it's easily considered spam by the moderators.

You can also embed the video on a web page and use standard web promotion tactics to send traffic to that page. And as you get external traffic, you'll notice that your videos do better and get higher rankings.

 Display your video above the fold. NEVER use autoplay.

OPTIMIZE - THE MAGIC SUCCESS FORMULA

When things aren't working, be smarter, not louder. (Sivers, 2020)[275]

Everything in the digital space, including online videos, leaves behind a trace of views, view times, and click-throughs. You owe it to yourself to constantly improve your video marketing tactics by analyzing how your videos perform on different channels. Only in this way will you get a better understanding of what types of video content work for your business and where you're finally gaining some traction.

A video marketer's job is never done!

When we talk about hustle, we mean consistency (Cannell & Travis, 2018)[276]:

- consistently creating and optimizing your content,
- consistently engaging with people,
- consistently improving.

When looking at the "optimize" category, think about what you want the platform to do for you and how you want to optimize the customer experience through your content.

Consider how the online video platform in question will let you optimize and map the different features in the customer journey or funnel. (Kane, 2020)[277]

So how can you optimize this flow? By looking at your video analytics.

- Pick the correct KPIs (growth in %) and metrics (watch time is the most important one).
- Analyze which tactics, formats, content, post times work best.
- Do more of what is working.
- Come up with new hypotheses for what doesn't appear to be working.

4.1 BRAND AWARENESS

Audiences on social media platforms communicate what they like through actions such as watch time, engagement, and clicks. The algorithm picks up on these social signals, improving the chances that your video gets recommended to more viewers.

But first, a tactic that is known and loved by growth hackers: A/B testing.

4.1.1 IMPROVE VIDEO AD PERFORMANCE WITH A/B TESTING

A/B testing, sometimes also called split testing, is a way to compare two versions of something to figure out which performs better. When applied to online advertising, it allows marketing professionals to experiment with different creatives, targeting, and calls-to-action of a video ad to decide on the video ad that guarantees the highest possible return on investment.

YouTube ads run on the Google AdSense network, and Instagram and Facebook video ads run on the Facebook advertising network. Both ad networks are highly sophisticated and provide advertisers with a plethora of behavioral data almost in real-time.

How-to for YouTube ads (in-stream ads):

1   Connect your YouTube channel to Google Ads (Linked Accounts). Approval may take some time (usually around 30 minutes).

2   Set up a remarketing list to start collecting data so you can create a similar audience in Google Ads manager. Audience: YouTube users.

3   Create campaign.

You'll need:

- URL of your YT ad video
- URL of your landing page.

Create a campaign without a goal > guidance > custom video campaign > set budget and dates (don't forget the end date!), e.g., $3/day (a good starting point to start collecting data).

- Bidding strategy: max CPV
- Inventory: all inventory (because your targeting is niche/narrow, quality of traffic is still good)
- Ad schedule: only specify when you learn from analytics WHEN you get most conversions
- Max CPV bid: 10 cents (a reasonable starting bid)

Create Ad Group 1, Ad Group 2, Ad Group 3 (with targeting based on three different parameters).

And wait for approval (24 hours to four business days).

But how do you know which targeting parameters to choose? Simple: by A/B testing.

Let's start with the set-up of our test campaign first.

In the first phase, target all demographics. Careful: always limit your campaigns to one country. If you want to target multiple countries, run multiple campaigns.

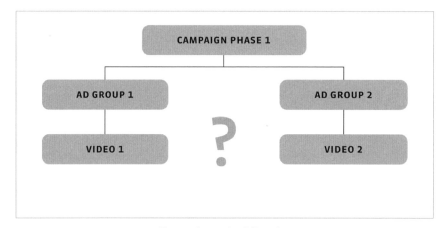

Phase 1 of campaign A/B testing

Now we're going to create two different Ad Groups, each with another video. The only parameter that makes the difference between these Ad Groups is the video ad creative.

Some examples of parameters you can change in the video creative:

- Video length:
    - Short (5-15 sec): Try looped videos similar to animated gifs or "cliffhanger" videos that encourage your audience to learn more.
    - Medium (~30 sec): Establish your point in the first 5 seconds, then drive it home. Strong examples include quick product overviews or "talking head" interviews.
    - Long (+1 min): Tell a richer story that makes an emotional connection or imparts knowledge (i.e., snippets from a recent webinar).
- The introductory text: Try calling out your audience.
- Different content in the video ad, for example, social proof: Try various customer testimonials to learn which resonate most with your audience.
- Landing experience: If you're collecting leads, test different landing pages to learn which web page drives higher conversions.

Let's imagine that video 1 performs better than video 2. Now duplicate this ad group and make some more variations of your video.

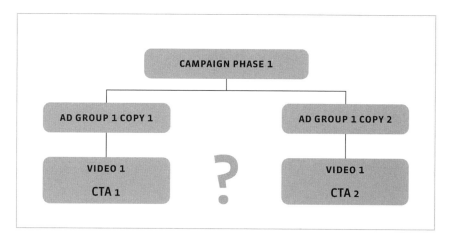

Phase 1 of campaign A/B testing: variations in CTA

Some examples of variations you can make in the CTA that goes with the video:

- Traffic to a landing page, e.g., register for an event
- Traffic to free call/consultation
- Traffic to e-commerce page with the low-price offer.

Let's imagine that CTA 1 performs better than CTA 2. Now duplicate this ad group and make some more variations of your video until you run out of options. For the sake of the exercise, imagine that it is video 1 that comes out as the winner once again.

In phase 2 of your campaign, the only difference in these Ad Groups is your audience targeting.

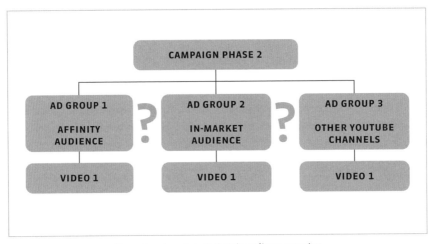

Campaign phase 2: variations in audience targeting

- Affinity Audience: Reach users based on what they're passionate about and their habits and interests.
- In-market Audience: Reach potential customers while they're actively browsing, researching, or comparing the types of products you sell. They are "in the market" for your products or services.
- "Other YouTube channels": This allows you to explore other YouTube channels your audience watches to garner a better understanding of what content resonates best with them.

Let's imagine that Ad Group 1, the one with Affinity Audience, shows the best results.

In phase 3 of your campaign A/B testing, the only parameter different in these ad groups is Category.

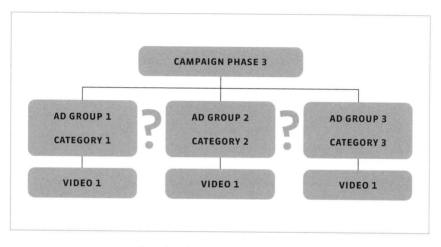

Campaign phase 3: variations in category

Now that you know which parameters for your Ad Groups and your Videos work best, you can set up your real campaign by copying your most successful Ad Group (and video).

Main settings:

- budget, e.g., $3 per day
- bidding strategy, e.g., max CPV (only charged when someone watches at least 30 seconds)
- networks: videos (if you're doing in-stream ads)
- locations: [country]
- inventory: e.g., all inventory (all the places where your video ad can display)
- frequency capping, e.g., 3 views per day
- targeting: categories from earlier research

Bidding strategies:

- To get website visits, bid by cost per 1,000 impressions (CPM)
- To collect leads, bid by cost per click (CPC)
- To get video views, bid by cost per view (CPV)
- To get more clicks for your budget, automate your bid (Automated bid)

IMPROVE ORGANIC IMPRESSIONS BY CREATING VIDEOS THAT ENGAGE

On video platforms, impressions highlight how many times your video thumbnails are shown on the video platform; think of impressions as indicating the number of opportunities your content was given to earn a view.

How can you give your videos the best head start? By creating videos that the social media algorithm loves. Videos that:

- Keep the users on the same platform as long as possible
- Elicit a lot of engagement in the form of likes, shares, and comments.

What about YouTube? YouTube does not have a social graph. Social graphs give social media platforms the ability to identify connections between consumers. Therefore, YouTube cannot recommend videos based on the viewing behavior of consumers' "friends" or recommend content users may like based on friends' activity, as done by other social media platforms such as Facebook and Instagram.

The YouTube search and discovery algorithm works in the background to match viewers to the videos they're most likely to watch and enjoy. (YouTube Creator Academy)[278] The recommendation system in YouTube takes various things into account. It analyzes user's history, their activities, geographical attributes, etc. For videos, they analyze its genre, thumbnails, content, description, aiming audience, subscribers, satisfaction count (likes, comments, shares), user surveys, etc. ((Daksh Trehan, 2021)[279]

The personal feed algorithm, first introduced by Facebook, was social media's solution to the sheer volume of short-form content that a human couldn't possibly process.

To avoid losing users' attention, algorithms are designed to find content that will engage unique users each time they come to the platform. (Kane, 2020)[280]

As you read posts recommended by the platform, it learns your preferences by tracking your behavior: what you choose to read, what you opt to dismiss, how long you spend on a piece of content, which articles you comment on, and which stories you choose to share. (Brennan, 2020)[281]

From the creator's perspective, TikTok's algorithms are most likely to reward your authenticity, creativity, and self-expression. (Olson, 2020)[282]

As TikTok put it, while "a video is likely to receive more views if posted by an account that has more followers, by virtue of that account having built up a larger follower base, neither follower count nor whether the account has had previous high-performing videos are direct factors in the recommendation system." (Wired, 2020)

Viewer engagement (likes, comments, dislikes, shares, embeds) in the first few hours after a video got posted is the not-so-secret ingredient of most social media algorithms.

 YouTube also offers dislikes. They're not nice to get but keep them: they will still help your rank.

After engagement, watch time is also a defining factor for video success. This is why longer videos do better most of the time - ideally 10:01-19:59 minutes, so there is enough space for monetization in the future). For some reason, the "2" of 20:00 minutes scares a lot of potential viewers off. Maybe they perceive 20 minutes of their time as too high a commitment?

 Don't make your video longer for the sake of more ad breaks. Never sacrifice quality for length.

Finally, using the latest features of the social media platform also helps boost your video's viral qualities. If this or that video platform just launched square, looping video stories, post lots of square, looping video stories. Feed the beast. Gary Vaynerchuk: "Every second you wait for something to happen, understand that the underpriced attention will become more expensive."

IMPROVE SOCIAL SIGNALS BY ASKING FOR ENGAGEMENT IN THE VIDEO

Connecting with your audience in engaging and meaningful ways is more important than ever.

Want more likes and subscribers? Just ask: "Like this video, subscribe to this channel, hit that notification button." Be real, honest, and genuine (it doesn't work if it feels forced). Tell them that engagement helps and that you appreciate it.

If you got value from this video
If you enjoy videos like these
... hit that like button ...
... ring the notification bell ...
... subscribe to my channel ...
... so you can find your way back more easily.
... so I can make more.
... so you don't miss a beat.

Ask for engagement in the middle of an items list, for example, and at the end of the video. Or use an overlay with these little sound effects (click, bell, ...).

Asking for comments works similarly. Ask open-ended questions. People love giving their opinion!

"What do you guys think? Let me know in the comments."

 Make tiny mistakes on purpose and let your commenters shine when they point them out to you in the comments. (*"Well, actually..."*)

IMPROVE ORGANIC WATCH TIME BY CREATING PLAYLISTS AND END SCREENS

YouTube is a highly competitive place. Millions of videos get uploaded every day, all of them vying for people's attention. You have 3-10 seconds max before viewers decide to continue watching or to bail out.

How engaging is the content of your video?

Watch time refers to the amount of time that viewers have spent watching your content and giving you a sense of what is being watched (instead of clicked on and then abandoned). Watch time is now more important than views. This metric is a good indicator of good quality content.

As you upload more videos, you can look at different Watch Time reports in YouTube Analytics to understand how well different videos perform. Watch Time is important because YouTube may surface your content to more people based on their viewing patterns. (YouTube Creator Academy)[283]

You can drop cards in the middle of the video, BUT they will drive people away from YouTube. Check your analytics and see where in your video your audience drops off. Then add cards a little before that point. Use it to link to another video of yours.

End screens allow you to extend watch time on your channel by directing viewers to up to four different elements during the last 20 seconds of your video.

- End screens are most successful when they give your viewers something relevant to watch; consider using them to drive traffic between episodes of your formats or series.
- Pair the video with a specific Call To Action (CTA) to maximize impact: End screens can be paired with an in-video "end card" that visually houses links and features a call to action directing viewers to "like, share, and subscribe."

Another way to accumulate more watch time for your channel (and to get suggested more frequently after viewing one of your videos) is playlists. Playlists, or channel shelves, provide an arranged viewing experience that can introduce content to your users. A playlist is an ordered list of videos that you create, often with a specific theme, that may appear in search results and suggested videos. This has several benefits:

- Viewers will watch more of *your* videos.
- Videos in the same playlist help each other rank higher.
- Videos in the same playlist are suggested as "next" more often.
- Adding a video to a playlist creates a new URL, like a signal to YouTube of new content.
- A lean-back experience: Grouping videos into playlists can provide a lean-back experience for your viewers.

4.1.5 IMPROVE CTR BY CREATING THUMB-STOPPING TITLES

The click-through rate (CTR) of your channel shows you what percentage of your impressions on YouTube turned into views; put simply, it is how often viewers click on a video title or thumbnail after seeing an impression.

Be clear, so YouTube knows what your video is about. Pick titles that will rank in both Search and Suggested. A title that describes what your video is about gives YouTube a definite topic so that the algorithm can suggest your video better. This will eventually lead to more views and more subscribers.

Thumb-stopping titles deliberately create a curiosity gap with viewers who are scrolling through their video feed.

When you use titles with words like *leaked, revealed, secret, exposed, unbelievable, solved, proof, debunked, caught on camera, you won't BELIEVE!* or *the TRUTH* (in caps) the line between a thumb-stopping video title and sheer clickbait becomes very thin.

Clickbait generally just means you create a curiosity gap that the video itself never resolves. Clickbait titles are attention grabs with little regard for the viewer. Use with caution!

 Go for titles that solve someone's problem.

4.1.6   **IMPROVE CTR BY CREATING THUMBNAILS THAT POP**

Thumbnails act as billboards for your content; they can capture viewers' visual attention and encourage them to engage with your content.

- Never be clickbait-y in your titles, but you can be in your thumbnail. Just make sure it is still relevant and show something that is in your video.
- Videos targeting your subscribers might highlight familiar features (like your face), while those targeting casual viewers can lean on more universally recognizable or appealing images.
- While stills from the video itself can work, taking some time during the production process to stage and shoot custom thumbnails for each video will save you a lot of time post-production.

IGTV also has thumbnails, titles, and descriptions. In the following chapters, however, we'll focus on YouTube.

YouTube thumbnail image design principles:

- Remove anything that makes the thumbnail image too crowded. Keep the bottom right corner free because that's where the time code goes.
- Showing faces and emotions: use a screenshot of your face with your most teasing expression.
- Pose for your thumbnail before you start recording and use this footage in your "blooper" reel at the end of your video. No matter who you are: you look like an idiot when posing for your thumbnail! Some YouTubers batch record their thumbnail poses in front of a green screen: serious, surprised, shocked, point left, point right, point up, point down.
- Color wheel opposites are pleasing to the eye.
- Use horizontal or vertical split-screen, for example, before and after, text vs. images.
- Branding and consistency are essential! Use Adobe Photoshop, Canva, GIMP, or even PowerPoint to create thumbnails that look like they belong together.

 If you want more attention paid to your thumbnails, discuss or reference well-known brands or celebrities. YouTube doesn't care much about copyright in thumbnail images (yet).

Never:

- Show something in your thumbnail that doesn't even appear in your video, for example, impossible animal fights.
- Use those damn red arrows and circles. It's not funny anymore.
- Show off your pretty girlfriend and her cleavage (doesn't work for boyfriends) or use titles that insinuate that you broke up with her (Better Marketing, 2020)[284]:
    - "We broke up" (with a picture of both of them crying in the thumbnail).
    - "He dumped me" (tears in thumbnail).
    - "Did we get back together?" (startled face, open mouth).
    - "We are still fighting" (them shouting at each other - but with Photoshopped red faces).
    - "I think I got my girlfriend pregnant last night" (oopsie face).
    - "I proposed. Did she say yes?" (startled face/open mouth, again)."

The text on your thumbnail is more triggering than the video title. Don't go overboard with the amount of text. You're designing for a mobile-first audience. This means small screens, limited bandwidth, and an "on the go" attitude.

Make the text on your thumbnail as easy to read as possible:

- Less is more: max three to four lines of text. Aim for less than four words.
- Use sans serif fonts like Helvetica.
- Capital letters are easier to read (but are sometimes perceived as SHOUTING).
- Use no more than two font types – any more is distracting.
- Avoid italics; they are harder to read.
- Use tacking or kerning: leave enough breathing space between your letters.
- Use 3D, depth (e.g., shadow effects), and bright colors like lime green or orange.
- The goal of a thumbnail is: make them stop scrolling and click.

 If you go to BuzzFeedVideo and sort by their most popular content, you'll find that every thumbnail either has a dollar figure on it, some delicious food, or hints at sex in some way.

IMPROVE TRAFFIC SOURCES BY IMPLEMENTING SEO BEST PRACTICES

You've created engaging, high-quality videos, but you're still losing them in Google's messy middle? Time to brush up on your SEO skills and apply them to your videos.

 ### REGULAR SEO (OFF-YOUTUBE)

Search Engine Optimization (SEO) is an integral part of many content marketing initiatives, and video is no different.

- Choose your platform wisely. No matter how popular they are, social media platforms tend to keep their content on their platform. This means that the more the app is used, the less the platform's content will appear in Google Search Results.
- This makes YouTube SEO's biggest secret. Since Google owns YouTube, videos rank highly in Google Search Engine Results Pages (SERPs). Many occupy the Featured Snippet box, with snippets selected algorithmically.
- Embed your videos on web pages and landing pages, and include a transcript for every video. The transcript acts as your page copy and helps you rank as search engines will know what that page is about. It also enables you to insert and rank for keywords. And as a bonus, transcripts make your page accessible to a larger audience.

YouTube is the second most popular search engine on the Internet because so many people use it as a resource for information. YouTube knows this, and they have developed a way to curate all uploaded videos and rank them in search results.

That's why YouTube SEO is a thing.

You can break up the process of YouTube SEO into three main components:

- Signals. Putting the right information in the right places for YouTube to rank your videos highly when people search for your keywords. We discussed these in Chapter 4.1

- Video content. Making a video that gives people the information they're looking for.
- Keywords. Analyzing the words people use to search for your topic.

In short, YouTube SEO is just like optimizing content for Google but based on YouTube ranking factors. (Biteable)[285]

In YouTube Analytics, Traffic Sources will give you a sense of how viewers are discovering your content; click through to get an in-depth view of each source (for example, what search terms are driving the most traffic to your video).

The three most important aspects of video SEO for YouTube are your title, description, and the tags you add to your video. Get these right, and your videos will start climbing the ranks. (Cannell & Travis, 2018)[286]

Step 1: Identify the most powerful keywords for your niche. There are a few ways to do this:

- Use autocomplete in YouTube's search bar. The results are ranked by demand volume.
- Tools like VidIQ and Tube Buddy help you analyze, for example, search volume and competing videos for your keywords. Look at the first few video results that already exist for these keywords. Analyze their title, description, tags, and how well they employ the key phrase. What are people saying? Are they asking any follow-up questions you can answer in your video? See what they are missing in terms of content.

Step 2: When you've defined your top three keywords, use answerthepublic. com to select a list of 10 questions that people ask around your top three keywords.

Step 3: Create a much more complete video series than what your competitors offer. This way, you can dominate highly trafficked videos.

A series of 30 videos is a good start. Why 30? This high volume of videos will create a constant stream of people who discover your channel through search. This increases the relevance of your channel for these keywords. Only then can you build enough trust to convert your audience to your product with a CTA.

How long will the effect of this series last? Long-tail lasts for five years (evergreen effect).

Note: all of the technical SEO optimizations come second. It all comes down to consistently answering your viewers' questions and creating good content for them.

YOUTUBE SEO IN VIDEO TITLE

YouTube video titles have a limit of 100 characters (also visually) to draw your audience in. Be brief: While YouTube allows up to 100 character titles, try keeping them under 70 characters and focusing on the most important words at the front.

Think in terms of users' searches: What will users be looking for? Make that the title. Hot topics should be within the first four words.

Titles on the longer side with more keywords might be better if you're still a small channel, but don't overdo it. The best titles are the ones that describe what is in the video. For example, the name of the person being interviewed, the title of the book you're reviewing, the brand name of the product you're discussing.

 Put the year in there if you can (except, of course, when it's evergreen content).

What works:

- Use numbers if you can: e.g., 6 Ways To Become A Social Media Expert
- Include a specific benefit: e.g., Triple Your Sales With These Simple Social Media Hacks
- Important words first (= front loading)
- Put one word in UPPERCASE
- Avoid offensive words or get blocked
- Ask questions
- Trending keywords
- Name dropping (famous brands/celebrities)

If you don't know which keywords and topics are popular within your space, you'll be creating videos on content that no one wants to watch or hear about.

Tools that can help with finding the right keywords to put in your video title:

- TubeBuddy (especially the Keyword Finder feature)
- VidIQ (more metrics and analytics)
- Neil Patel's Ubersuggest is a free tool that'll show you what keywords are popular.
- answerthepublic.com

YOUTUBE SEO IN VIDEO DESCRIPTION

The description box is not only where the conversion happens but also a powerful keyword injection zone. People spend all this time creating a great video and then don't take one minute to write a short description.

 The description box has a 1,000 character limit. Use wordcounter.net to adapt your text until you get it right. Write a description that:

- Is a good summary of the video
- Contains potential keywords, key phrases, and variations in natural language
- Will help in the long run for evergreen
- Points to a more extended or complete version of the content, e.g., blog post.

Your description needs to have five parts, and it must be in this order (Clarke, 2019)[287]:

1   A hyperlink to your website. This must be first and must include the http://.... Example: https://clowillaerts.com. Just as with newsletters, the CTR on links in this box goes down after the first one. Put your most important URL here. In all, don't put more than five URLs in your description.

2   Reiterate the incredible offer or CTA you made in the video. "Head over to clowillaerts.com for one hour of free digital marketing consulting."

3   Main content of your video. You are given 1,000 characters here. Use as much of that as you can. Include what they will be learning in your video. If you're not sure what to write about, simply talk about WHY you feel the video topic is so important. And then give summaries of the steps/topics you cover in the video.

4   This is the part "below the fold" to paste the default part of your description. If you have a Facebook page, Twitter account, ... whatever... put it here. This may include other social network links, playlists of related videos, subscription links, and more. (Remember to include the http:// part.)

5   Add your primary call to action with a URL. Example: "Don't forget to visit https://clowillaerts.com for one hour of free digital marketing consulting."

Use emojis to capture attention for specific links. Emojis and links are there to help your viewers scan the description text. Keep them below five.

YOUTUBE SEO IN VIDEO TAGS

Another metadata field that is often overlooked by video uploaders contains the tags. Tags consist of *keywords*, not key phrases.

- The first tags you fill in include the keywords from your title. Example: "Video Marketing."
- Use enough tags to thoroughly and accurately describe the video. Focus on information not communicated in your title and description.
- If you're making a series of videos, just copy-paste them from your previous ones. Help organize content read by machines, less by humans (those who read the description).
- Include a mix of both general ("course", "tips", "Instagram") and specific ("Instagram video monetization") tags. Super broad tags don't work 99% of the time, so you might just as well spare yourself the effort. Specific tags are the words that someone would type in as a search query.
- Use tags to build playlists. You can automatically add videos to a playlist with video tags.

 Find a video that is similar to yours and just copy their tags. Don't be afraid to use the same tags your competitors are using! It's a marketing best practice that's been used by many.

Which tools to use?

- TubeBuddy makes a huge difference. It helps you keep below the character limit and shows the ranks of these keywords and related keyword suggestions. Keyword explorer: play around with keyword phrases until you hit green.
- Google Trends and Google Ads Keyword Planner will help! These tools help identify popular keywords and their synonyms; including these terms can help maximize traffic from search.

OTHER YOUTUBE SEO FACTORS

Say your keyword phrases throughout the video. YouTube's speech recognition algorithm is getting better and better at speech-to-text. It does so to get a better idea of what the video is about.

This ability is also used to add CC (Closed Captions) to your video. YouTube is pretty good at picking up what you're saying in the videos, but it's not 100%. So unless you upload your transcript, your video will not rank as high, and you will not get as many views.

How can you activate closed captions and subtitles on YouTube? In Creator Studio, pick "English (automatic)" as the CC option. Give it some time. You can edit these afterward if there are any mistakes.

By uploading the corrected transcript, you're also optimizing your video for Voice search. Voice search, also called voice-enabled, allows the user to use a voice command to search the Internet, a website, or an app. In a broader definition, voice search includes open-domain keyword queries on any information on the Internet, such as Google Voice Search, Cortana, Siri, and Amazon Echo.

4.3 IMPROVE CONVERSION TO SALES CHANNEL BY OPTIMIZING YOUR SALES VIDEO

Remember the short and snappy Sales Video with the heartbeat narrative structure? Now turn that heartbeat narrative up to eleven for this heart-attack-inducing super charged Sales Video.

4.3.1 REMOVE LAST-MINUTE OBJECTIONS WITH A SUPERCHARGED SALES VIDEO

Below is an extreme example of a sales video outline that speeds up the buying decision process by taking away as many cognitive biases as possible. The fact that the entire video is a call-to-action (to buy the product) makes it a sales video.

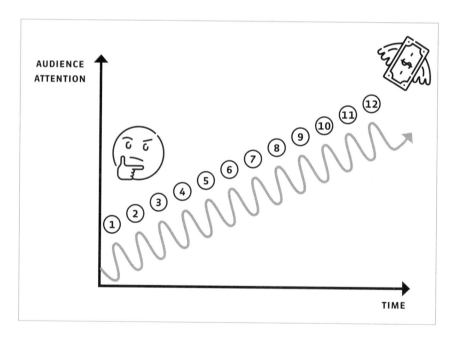

Audience attention vs. sales video time

Outline for a promotional video:

1 CONNECT Start by making an emotional connection – resonate with the viewer by addressing the pain points you know they feel. Talk specifically about their obstacles, problems, and challenges.

   a *"You know how …"*

   b *"Do you want X?"*

   c *"Do you dream of X? But feel like Y?"* (the reason they think they can't).

   d *"Do you dream of X? But find that Y?"* (the problem they face when they try).

2 RELATE to their problems by telling a story about your own life experience.

   a STRUGGLE *"I get it because I went through that too."* Tell your audience your struggle.

   b SEARCH Tell your audience about your search for solutions to your struggle (A).

   c Tell them how you solved the problem for yourself. Name the break-through that led to the C (the success).

   d SUCCESS Talk about your success and how your life changed with your success.

3 SOLUTION Become the solution to their problems – cause intrigue by showing that you can solve the users' problems.

   a *"Well, what we do is …"*

   b *"This one system to follow"*

   c *"This set of steps to follow"*

   d *"If you had this mindset, you'll have success as I have."*

4   FEATURES Tell them how their life will change and how their family's life will change. Then, describe the features. The features could be immediate access to video training or a workbook - so that they can accomplish X (less debt, more passive income, a healthier lifestyle).

5   VALUE Never tell them the price first. Tell them the value first. Make the value more significant than the price. The bigger the ask, the more you need to explain the value you offer and the more you rely on trust.

6   USP Whose problem are you solving, better than all the others in the field? Not only should you tell potential customers what it is you're offering, but you must also tell them what it is about your company/brand/product that differentiates you from your competitors.

7   BONUS / FREEBIE The bonus If you buy (this system/ebook/these steps),

   a   *"We're going to throw in X."* Make the bonuses as good as the first thing you're selling.

8   SOCIAL PROOF Now add testimonials from people who are enjoying what you're selling and love it. If you're just starting and you have no testimonials because no one knows who you are yet, enlist a cousin, friend, or neighbor.

9   FOMO "Only today"

   a   *"Click the button below because there are only ten (ebooks, guides, training videos) left for sale."*

   b   *"Click the button below now; this offer is only available for 20 more hours."*

   c   *"I'm not going to tell you about this product again."*

10 SURPRISE Casually drop another bonus and roll more testimonial videos.

   a   *"Oh, I forgot to tell you, this offer includes this free ebook to help you do X."*

11 CTA to get them off YouTube to your owned media.

    a   Online: follow, subscribe, register, download, buy, order.

    b   Offline: call, visit.

12 GUARANTEE Give a 30-day money-back guarantee and make sure you give a buyer back their money when they ask for it. Always honor a guarantee.

MAKE VIDEO CONTENT BASED ON PRODUCT TRENDS

This one is a bit of a growth hack.

Hunt the web for products that people are enthusiastic about: they are open to video content that helps them find these products. Find a product or consumer trend you can tie into your products or services and use the product name as the "hook" for your video.

- TrendWatching: TrendWatching is an independent trend firm that scans the globe for the most promising consumer trends and insights. TrendWatching has a team of professionals in London, New York, São Paulo, Singapore, Sydney, and Lagos who report worldwide trends. (shopify.com/blog 2020)[288]
- Trend Hunter: Trend Hunter is the world's largest, most popular trend community. Fuelled by a global network of 137,000 members and 3,000,000 fans, Trend Hunter is a source of inspiration for aspiring entrepreneurs and the insatiably curious.
- The easiest way to find trending products online is to check Google Trends. The Google Trends tool examines the popularity of top search queries in Google across various regions and languages. It will show you the trends of your product ideas based on search volume from 2004 onward. (shopify.com/blog 2020)[289]
- Shut Up And Take My Money subreddit: Interesting, innovative, useful products that people want badly. (shopify.com/blog 2020)[290]
- Google Trends for Google Shopping[291]: The chances are that everybody wants the latest PlayStation or iPhone, but dig deeper.

4.4 MONETIZE YOUR VIDEOS

There are three ways to make money from your videos:

1   By monetizing your videos

2   By monetizing your community Chapter 4.5

3   By monetizing your video skills Chapter 4.6

4.4.1 MONETIZE YOUR VIDEOS BY OPTIMIZING FOR AD REVENUE

Video monetization is the process of generating income through the videos you share online on any platform. This is usually achieved through advertising, subscriptions, or direct transactions. (Uscreen, 2019) [292]

The YouTube Partner Program is one of the most well-known platforms that allow video creators to monetize their channel. There is, however, a particular threshold for YouTubers who want to participate (YouTube Creator Academy)[293]:

- Having a minimum of 1,000 subscribers and an accumulated 4,000 hours of watch time on your videos (=at least viewed for 50%)
- Successfully getting reviewed for brand safety.
- Having collected a minimum amount of $100 in ad revenue before YouTube starts paying you the 55% revenue split
- And if you want to enable multiple mid-roll ads, your video must be at least eight minutes long.

In some cases, creators can also act as their salespeople in their negotiations with advertisers or sponsors.

 Check which of your videos earn you the most money. Make more videos with this type of content.

To optimize for revenue from video monetization, your channel needs to strike a balance between:

- Engaging a large and active community of viewers and commenters,
- Providing high-quality, advertiser-friendly video content regularly,
- Creating monetizable content, i.e., around topics bound to attract video ads with a high CPM (Cost Per Measurement - usually 1,000 views).
- To enable mid-roll ads, a minimum length of eight minutes. The more ad breaks, the more YouTube will recommend the video. For longer videos, adding multiple ad breaks is a delicate balance between pleasing the YouTube gods and annoying your viewers.

 Watch your upload video like a viewer to decide where to insert an ad break, e.g., right before you deliver, just after a mini cliff-hanger.

The following categories are associated with the highest viewability for videos on YouTube (Think With Google)[294]:

- Games 82%
- Business & Industrial 72%
- Internet & Telecom 72%
- Shopping 72%
- Arts & Entertainment 71%
- Science 71%

The top highest paid AdSense keywords for 2021 (by industry/niche) are (Source: Alejandro Rioja)[295]:

- Insurance $61 CPC
- Gas/Electricity $58 CPC
- Loans $50 CPC
- Mortgage $46 CPC
- Attorney $48 CPC
- Lawyer $42 CPC
- Donate $42 CPC
- Conference Call $42 CPC

Nine-year-old Ryan Kaji earned $29.5m as 2020's highest-paid YouTuber.

This looks like easy money, but don't forget you're dependent on the platform's rules and regulations. If you break them, your videos can be demonetized, or even worse: you can get de-platformed.

To avoid de-platforming:

- Make sure you adhere to the YouTube Guidelines as failure to do so could result in loss of privileges and, in extreme cases, channel closure.
- After receiving a warning for your first offense, each following violation will result in a strike. If you receive three strikes within 90 days, you may risk having your channel shut down permanently.

Remember that your "offline" actions may also impact your channel's performance and reputation.

*In 2018, YouTube suspended radio host Alex Jones's channel for 90 days for violating
hate speech and graphic content policies. They later terminated his channel
permanently in 2019.*

YouTube demonetization is when videos or channels lose their ability to earn
advertising income. This is often due to changes in YouTube's algorithm or
response to requests by advertisers to be removed.

With the steady increase in extremist content and fake news, some advertising
risks getting displayed next to objectionable content. From the side of the
advertisers, this is called a lack of brand safety. YouTubers tend to describe it as
the Adpocalypse. During the first Adpocalypse in 2019, small creators saw their
income from advertising disappear. Many have switched to Twitch as a leading
source of income and found it brought them closer to their community.

YouTube is not the only platform that offers a share of ad revenue with its
creators. Approved Twitch Partners can earn a percentage of the revenue
generated from any (mid-roll) ads played on their channel.

Facebook also offers monetization of your video and stories; there were also
plans for IGTV monetization, but its current status is unclear. (Facebook For
Business)[296]

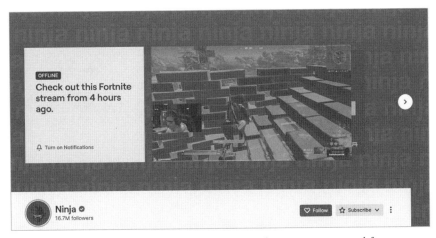

The most popular streamer on Twitch, Ninja, earns at least $100,000 per month from
Twitch alone.

Spotify Podcast creators also have Monetization options:

- Insert mid-roll ads: "add a sponsored segment" between the segments of your podcast episode.
- Sponsorships: create an ad for Spotify but put your spin on it. Activate this in all of your episodes!

 MONETIZE YOUR VIDEOS BY OPTIMIZATION FOR SPONSORSHIP OR FUNDING

Once you've garnered a substantial following on the platform, you'll likely have organizations reach out to you and request you to promote or review their products in exchange for cash. Be careful when doing this: your audience is well aware of when something is being advertised.

On YouTube, creators can activate the "Includes Paid Promotion" disclaimer tag. This tag appears in the bottom left corner of a video for the first few seconds that viewers watch.

 Only promote products that you're genuinely interested in, and you think will be valuable for your audience, too - that'll keep your engaged viewers happy.

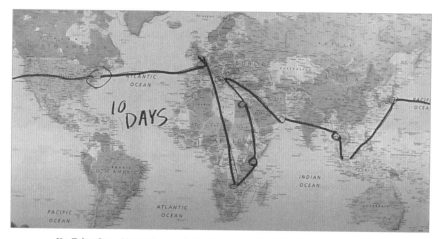

YouTuber Casey Neistat has worked with sponsors like Nike, Mercedes, J. Crew, and Samsung.

For the larger channels, YouTube offers Brand Connect, which enables creators to negotiate who will advertise.

Eligible Facebook Pages can make use of the "Brand Collabs Manager." Brand Collabs Manager makes it easier to get discovered for paid partnerships and unlock the earning potential of your Facebook presence. Connect with brands looking to promote their products and services through the relationship you have with your followers and then collaborate on campaigns to increase your engagement. (Facebook for Creators)[297]

Other video platforms fund some of their most prized creators directly from a creators fund.

TikTok adopted a tried and tested Chinese strategy, setting up a "Creators fund" to subsidize influencers who met specific criteria. (Brennan, 2020)[298]

Later in 2020, Snapchat announced the launch of "Spotlight," an additional tab highlighting the best videos submitted by Snapchat creators - and pay them for it from a creator fund. (newsroom.snap.com)

In May 2021, YouTube announced YouTube Shorts Fund, a $100M fund distributed over the course of 2021-2022. (YouTube Official Blog)[299]

REPACKAGE YOUR EDUCATION VIDEOS AND SELL THEM AS AN ONLINE COURSE

Joeparys.com positions himself as "the bestselling online instructor".

As soon as you've made a series of at least 15 educational videos about a particular topic, you can repackage these videos as an online course and create passive income.

Add:

- course intro
- wrap-up
- bonus lecture
- "walking side notes" in a more casual (e.g., vlogging) format

Then, select a third-party delivery platform for these courses. A few possibilities are:

- Udemy is an American massive open online course provider aimed at professional adults and students. Careful: you can't sell your course on, e.g., Udemy if the same videos are still available for free on YouTube. This might harm your instructor profile.
- Teachable is an all-in-one course hosting platform that allows you to collect payments, deliver your course and offer special price promotions.
- Coursera is an American massive open online course provider.

- Skillshare is an American online learning community for people who want to learn from educational videos. The courses, which are not accredited, are available through subscription.

If you don't want to be dependent on third parties, refer to your website for the online course. Send people to the same spot (online course, buy book) all the time.

 Video overlay: don't show your logo - show your URL!

Use WordPress (content management system) with WooCommerce (e-commerce) and LearnDash (clean lecture videos hosted on Vimeo pro for a smooth watching experience).

 Sell your course in a bundle or package with other products or services so you can charge more.

Example: $297 for:

- A course with a minimum of 15 videos
- PDFs with templates and exercises
- A handbook or workbook
- Video calls with coaches
- A Facebook group for answering questions

If done right, you can turn this Facebook Group into the central delivery platform for your Community of Interest. Interest-based paid communities provide expert feedback, exclusive resources, and community support for those with shared interests or challenges. (Andreessen-Horowitz, 2020)[300]

How to promote your online course:

1 Sample some of your educational video content for free on video and social media platforms.

 Add a 10-second introduction to the full monty – "This is part of an online course" – and add the CTA at the end.

2 Promote these free course samples. For example: run discovery ads for those not in-stream, or Google Ads for YouTube videos for $2/day or $5/day.

3   Organize and promote a free webinar. To boost your online course, organize a free webinar. List this online event on Eventbrite and push it with a targeted Facebook, YouTube, or LinkedIn video ads campaign.

For the webinar itself, use Zoom. Make sure that you record the webinar to the cloud. Repurpose this recording later for promotional clips on social media platforms.

The webinar itself is a 90-minute long promotion of you and your product or service (in this case: the online course).

Webinar structure:

1   Introduction/hook: hook viewers in to stay for the entire webinar. Become relatable by telling your personal story.

2   The training itself. Keep it simple and deal with the three biggest objections or deal-breakers that potential customers come up with.

3   Close / sale / release. Time to introduce your insanely valuable offer - impossible to say no. Use scarcity, bonus material, and testimonials.

4   Fundamental principles when running this webinar:

1   You sell results, not a product.

2   Why should they commit to your process to get it (your XYZ plan)? Throw rocks at the competition.

3   Do they believe they can do it? Dumb it down. Take the complexity away.

4   Do they believe they can do it in 30-45 days?

4.5 MONETIZE YOUR COMMUNITY

Find your 1,000 true fans. They alone could create a sustainable business for you. People come for the content, but stay for the connection! Their trust and engagement enable you to create a consistent income. (Cannell & Travis, 2018)[301] These will be the people who will:

- watch each of your videos,
- support your video production in every way they can,
- and purchase every product you launch.

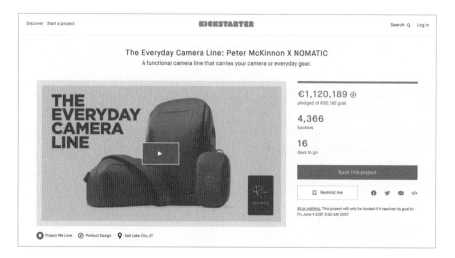

Peter McKinnon's audience is primarily photographers and filmmakers. When McKinnon and Nomatic launched two camera bags with a Kickstarter campaign, they reached the goal of $100,000 in 20 minutes.

Online viewers are unlikely to pay directly for your videos, but if they can relate to you, they are willing to pay for the privilege of belonging to your community. People love being part of your journey. After that, your growth will be exponential.

Tactics that help you grow and foster your community:

- Celebrate achievements
- For maximum engagement: respond with video in YT stories or even comments
- Tag or mention people or businesses (especially if you want to become a brand ambassador)
- Community management via a Discord server, a Facebook Group, or a Slack Channel
- Organize Live Q&As and webinars
- Build your email list for special announcements

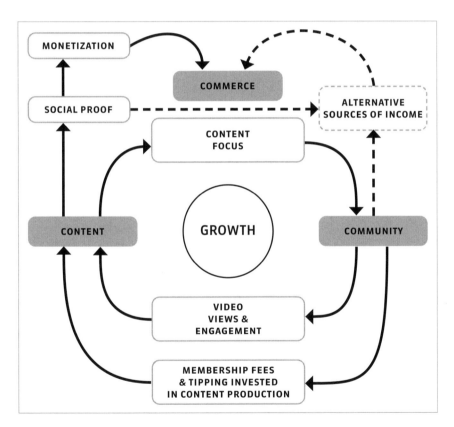

The content-community-commerce flywheel

How can you set this content-community-commerce flywheel in motion?

1   Create content that appeals to them (and them alone). Example: instead of creating a channel on "YouTube marketing," make one on "YouTube marketing for local business owners."

2   Listen carefully to your audience's demands. Use YouTube analytics to figure out the type of videos your audience likes, and find out where your audience's attention drops.

3   Validate demand and launch a product: Along the way of listening to your audience for creating your videos, ask them what they are willing to pay for.

4   Example: Maybe they want you to organize an event or launch an online course on one of their pain points. Research, validate their demand, then give your audience what they want.

5   Add more ways of monetization into the mix. Once you find something your audience likes, repeat the process to include more ways to monetize your community.

In 2020 North Carolina-based YouTube creator Jimmy Donaldson, aka MrBeast, launched the MrBeast Burger fast-food chain in locations where his YouTube analytics showed many of his community members lived.

4.5.1 **TIPPING, DONATIONS, AND MICRO-TRANSACTIONS**

Most video platforms allow viewers to reward creators – often livestreamers – with payments through the platform (and the platform takes a cut). (Andreessen-Horowitz, 2020)[302]

Broken Window Theory is the passion project of Till and Marco, two friends from Germany who explore abandoned places and seek beauty in decay. In 2020, they used money donated by their community donations to buy a new drone camera.

 Ask your viewers to support directly and clearly. Explain how their support helps you produce more or level up.

These payments can be one-off, monthly, or occasional micro-payments during live events. For anyone wondering how to make money from YouTube Super Chat, the key is to organize and promote livestreams. Promote them in videos, other social media platforms, and anywhere else where your audience loves hanging out.

- YouTube monetization rates for Super Chat range from $1 to $500, and the company takes a 30% cut from the revenue. YouTube Superchat lets the audience of a livestream buy chat messages that stand out and, in certain instances, pin them to the top of the comments section of a livestream. YouTube Viewer Applause allows the viewer to send a $2 tip to the creator in real-time.
- Facebook has added a feature to give creators a new way to earn money and fans to show appreciation. With Stars, viewers of Facebook live video can support content creators in real-time. (Facebook Blueprint course)[303]

4.5.2 PAID MEMBERSHIP

Channel or VIP Subscriptions are examples of content that is structurally funded by the fans. Audiences pay directly for exclusive access to content, community, or the creator.

The most famous example is Patreon.

Patreon is an American membership platform that provides business tools for content creators to run a subscription service. It helps creators and artists earn a monthly income by offering rewards and perks to their subscribers. Patreon was co-founded in May 2013 by Jack Conte of the band Pomplamoose, when they received a YouTube AdSense cheque for the million views they received for a creatively shot music video for one of their tracks. It cost $10,000 to film. The return on investment for Conte and his wife, Nataly Dawn, the other half of the band? Around $150. (Stokel-Walker, 2018)[304] Strictly speaking, Patreon is not a membership site: several people pay you a small amount every month to keep making more videos. The average amount patrons contribute per month OR per project pledge is $6.70. Fans are paying an average of $12 per month. If 200 people each pay $15 a month, this is $3,000/month. Easy money? Not quite: you have to keep delivering value. On the upside, Patreon is already a proven concept. The amounts are not life-changing but still more than you would make through YouTube Ad Revenue. BUT you have to keep delivering value every month.

These offer either direct platform subscriptions or creator subscriptions on the platform (and the platform takes a cut or charges a monthly fee). (Andreessen-Horowitz, 2020)[305]

Some other examples of membership platforms are Substack, OnlyFans, BuyMeACoffee, Cameo, Ko-Fi and SubscribeStar.

Most of the creators deliver their membership programs from external platforms and promote their central video presence (like their YouTube channel, Facebook Page, or Twitch stream).

More prominent players like YouTube and even TikTok try to incentivize their creators to run their membership programs without leaving the platform.

Twitch channel subscriptions are a small, recurring donation to the creator (minus a cut for Twitch). During the livestreams, the community is very active in the chatbox and is delighted when the streamer responds to what they read there.

On YouTube, the Community tab is available to all YouTube creators with over 1,000 subscribers. (YouTube Creator Academy)[306]

This YouTube feature allows you to socially engage your audience away from the videos and content you upload. You can do this by:

- interacting with viewers in the Comments section of videos
- hosting livestreams for your loyal fans
- making videos requested by your community, or
- sharing extra content via the Community tab
- posting status updates and subscriber polls
- hosting live Q&A and AMA ("Ask Me Anything") sessions

When your YouTube channel gets more than 30,000 subscribers, you can add another income stream by leveraging channel memberships. Fans pay $4.99 a month for a membership package that includes perks like:

- early access to videos
- members-only live chat
- exclusive emojis, and more

E-COMMERCE AND SOCIAL SHOPPING

Shopify and other commerce tools and platforms enable creators to recommend and sell products through features such as livestreaming and live virtual auctions. (Andreessen-Horowitz, 2020)[307]

These products can be either physical or digital goods.

Creators produce free content to capture and shift attention to owned products and services like:

- courses
- books
- downloadables
- apps
- consulting
- coaching
- workshops
- physical products
- capital and deal flow

Example platforms:

- Shopify is an online store builder trusted by over 1,000,000 stores.
- Gumroad is an online platform that facilitates the sale of products by creators directly to consumers.
- Luma provides a platform for people to host virtual classes, record live shows, educate, and find their communities via Zoom.
- Sellfy is an all-in-one e-commerce service designed for creators to sell digital or physical products, digital subscriptions, or print-on-demand merchandise online.
- Bandcamp's mission is to create the best possible service for artists and labels to share and earn money from their music and fans to discover and enjoy it.

As an end product, videos are incredibly versatile. Videos are also a prime example of digital products. If you sell digital products, margins are higher than in the physical world. Plus, your customers get instant gratification: they can start using them immediately after buying.

Other examples of digital goods are virtual items, in-platform upgrades, or premium services. (Andreessen-Horowitz, 2020)[308]

"2 Hours Doing Nothing", a video of Indonesian YouTuber Muhammad Didit staring into his camera and doing nothing for two hours, achieved 1.7 million views on the day of release and 3 million in one month. The video was later adapted to a mobile game.

If you're already running an e-commerce business, it's a great idea to run a video channel in addition to this store. Use video marketing to promote your store and your products in both your videos and your descriptions.

Plenty of YouTubers capitalize on their personal connection with their fans to sell additional items, on top of receiving AdSense income and sponsorship money from brands. (Stokel-Walker, 2018)[309] Example: Jake Paul and Logan Paul.

 If you haven't already set up your store, use Shopify or Magento to set up your store.

Once you've got your store up and running, you can sell products related to your YouTube channel:

- Your own branded merch
- Products that you've mentioned in your videos, or
- Items that you think your viewers will be interested in.

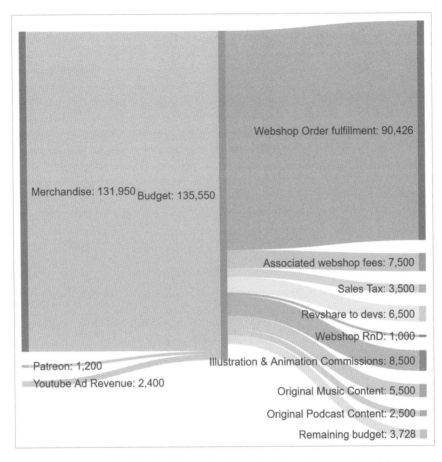

In 2019, YouTuber Kaiser Cat Cinema shared the split of the yearly revenue he made by selling merchandise, running a webshop, Patreon, and YouTube ad revenue.[310]

Careful: These products offer lower margins – especially if you keep shipping and handling costs in mind. Some viewers may also consider this as a sign that you're "selling out."

 Teespring is integrated into your YouTube channel: the products are shown immediately below your video.

More mushrooms **#fyp** #art #diy ▷ 24.7K 2020-8-14

She's had enough of me #fyp ▷ 12K 2020-8-14

Hope you guys like it! :) **#fyp #art #painting**... ▷ 81.4K 2020-8-13

A TikTok user who has been soaring to new heights is 21-year-old Jordyn, with the TikTok account bydroj. She is an artist who began making art prints for T-shirts and tops via TikTok. (Olson, 2020)[331]

4.5.4 **AFFILIATE MARKETING**

With affiliate marketing, you make an affiliate commission or a flat finder's fee from sales to your audience.

The most well-known is the Amazon Associate program for products/services that you recommend.

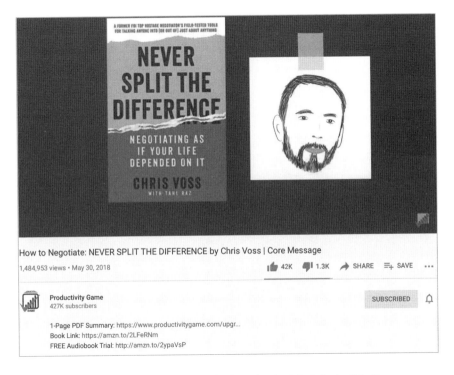

With each book summary on its YouTube channel and website[312], Productivity Game
provides Amazon affiliate links to the titles that are being discussed.

A variation on this theme is CPA marketing (Cost per Action - usually an email opt-in). Your audience signs up as a lead (not necessarily a paying customer).

Commissions don't tend to be very high, but there's a lower barrier to entry. Example: via TubeBuddy (up to 50%, e.g., hosting services).

 Open an account on networks like CJ Affiliate, ShareASale, and Rakuten LinkShare as soon as you start your YouTube channel. It might take a while to start seeing enough video views to translate into any actual sales, but affiliate marketing can eventually become a big chunk of your income.

4.5.5 TICKETED COMMUNITY EVENTS

Virtual Live Experiences: Facilitating "ticketed" shows, one-on-one interactions, or group meetups. (Andreessen-Horowitz, 2020)[313]

VidCon is a multi-genre online video tech conference, held annually since 2010 in Southern California and currently organized by ViacomCBS. It was founded by You-Tubers Hank Green and John Green, also known as the Vlogbrothers. Photo by Gage Skidmore[314]

4.6 MONETIZE YOUR SKILLS

Spending money to learn a new skill gives you leverage on yourself. This handbook helps you to use video marketing like a pro. What's next?

4.6.1 SET UP YOUR VIDEO PRODUCTION BUSINESS

Your videos are, in fact, demos of your video production skills. (InfluencerMarketingHub)[315]

 This is where Vimeo shines! Show, don't tell. Upload your showreels to Vimeo to come into contact with future employers.

"All of a sudden we were going from a rinky-dink, three-person team to a mini Netflix. It's a total game-changer." Rob Young, Founder, Prodigies. (Vimeo Blog, 2020)[316]

Business idea 1: produce custom videos.

Create a package for five videos delivered in 30 days. Each video consists of:

- 7-minute long video
- 50+ word title
- 300-word description
- 2 sponsor links
- 25 tags
- 1 thumbnail price

 Make sure that you always have the following on any contract with a sponsor: price, payment method (schedule), number of revisions, and whether or not you are willing to reshoot your video.

Many businesses and independent creators learn how to sell streaming videos online by distributing their content through a video subscription platform (also called an OTT platform because it goes "over the top" of traditional broadcast television). (Vimeo Blog, 2020)[317]

4.6.2 USE VIDEO MARKETING TO LAUNCH A DIGITAL BUSINESS

YouTube is a marketing machine! For example, if you make how-to videos with plumbing tips, this will lead to new customers for your plumbing business.

How do you attract real-world customers from YouTube? By collecting qualified leads for your business.

1 Convert them to your "link sending" vehicle. Take them off YouTube to your owned media. The vehicle can be:

   a An email list. Get their permission to email them, for example, by organizing a free webinar via Eventbrite or offering a pdf with exclusive bonus material ("The Ultimate Guide to X") or recipes.

   b A Facebook Group

   c A Facebook Messenger Subscriber list (this has a 90% open rate for links you send them!)

      Use ManyChat broadcasting software to message all your subscribers at once. Example: promotions and hard CTAs like "50% off - only today".

Neil Patel uses his YouTube videos to attract customers for his digital marketing agency.

2 Run retargeting ads on YouTube pre-roll or Facebook and lead them to your "Money Maker": a sales or landing page and checkout pages. These pages are the only thing that converts trust into money.

3 Keep your funnel as simple as possible. Keep continuity in branding throughout your entire funnel – otherwise, people get confused and leave.

4 Use your "link sending" vehicle to send them back to YouTube or your podcast series or owned media.

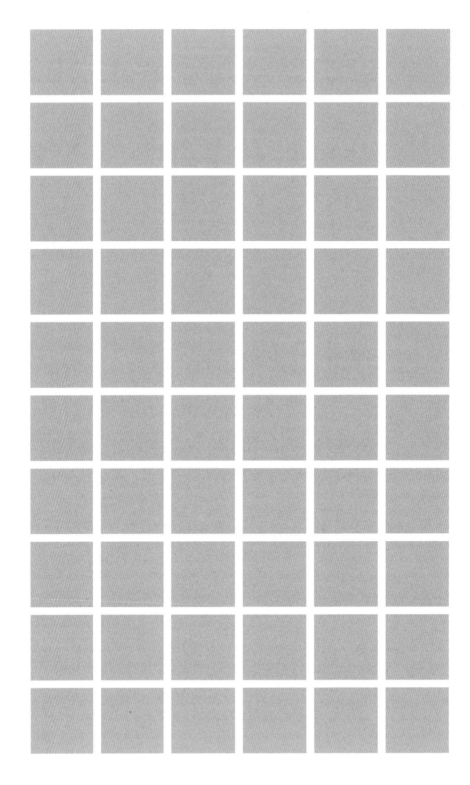

ENDNOTES

1   2020 Video Trends & Usage: Consumption Is up 120% During COVID-19 https://wistia.com/learn/marketing/covid-19-video-trends

2   YouTube is social media's big winner during the pandemic https://www.cnbc.com/2021/04/07/youtube-is-social-medias-big-winner-during-the-pandemic.html

3   Why We're Feeling Digital Video https://www.thinkwithgoogle.com/consumer-insights/consumer-trends/trending-data-shorts/digital-video-streaming-data

4   Turning to Learning to Adapt to Our New Realities https://blog.linkedin.com/2020/april-/21/turning-to-learning-to-adapt-to-our-new-realities

5   How people use YouTube for learning https://www.thinkwithgoogle.com/consumer-insights/how-people-use-youtube-for-learning/

6   How COVID-19 changed the way people work, by Kaspersky https://media.kasperskydaily.com/wp-content/uploads/sites/92/2020/05/03191550/6471_COVID-19_WFH_Report_WEB.pdf

7   Live Video Is Replacing In-Person Interactions https://www.emarketer.com/content/live-video-is-replacing-in-person-interactions

8   Video Advertising Worldwide https://www.statista.com/outlook/dmo/digital-advertising/video-advertising/worldwide

9   Content, Consumption, and Culture: Perspectives From the Entertainment Industry https://www.facebook.com/business/news/insights/content-consumption-and-culture-perspectives-from-the-entertainment-industry

10 Coronavirus video trends https://www.thinkwithgoogle.com/consumer-insights/corona-virus-video-trends/

11 What Is Content Marketing? https://contentmarketinginstitute.com/what-is-content-marketing/

12 Google Trending Data Shorts: "Why We're Feeling Digital Video" https://www.thinkwithgoogle.com/consumer-insights/consumer-trends/trending-data-shorts/digital-video-streaming-data

13 *YouTube for Business: Online Video Marketing for Any Business*, by Michael Miller

14 How to create a compelling video ad for every stage of the customer journey https://www.thinkwithgoogle.com/future-of-marketing/creativity/youtube-video-ad-creative/

15 *YouTubers: How YouTube Shook Up T.V. and Created a New Generation of Stars*, by Chris Stokel-Walker (Canbury Press, 2019)

16   SMT Expert Roundup: The Future of TikTok https://www.socialmediatoday.com/news/smt-expert-roundup-the-future-of-tiktok/565714/

17   How to create an effective video ad for every stage of the customer journey https://www.thinkwithgoogle.com/future-of-marketing/creativity/youtube-video-ad-creative/

18   8.1 The History of Movies https://saylordotorg.github.io/text_understanding-media-and-culture-an-introduction-to-mass-communication/s11-01-the-history-of-movies.html

19   The University of Chicago, Theories of Media, Video https://csmt.uchicago.edu/glossary2004/video.htm

20   Cisco Visual Networking Index (VNI) Complete Forecast Update, 2017–2022 https://newsroom.cisco.com/press-release-content?type=webcontent&articleId=1955935

21   Online video viewing to reach 100 minutes a day in 2021, by Publicis Media's Zenith unit https://s3.amazonaws.com/media.mediapost.com/uploads/ZenithOnlineVideoForecast.pdf   Sourced from Time Spent Watching Online Video Expanding To 100 Minutes Daily, Ad Budgets Set To Follow   https://www.mediapost.com/publications/article/340714/time-spent-watching-online-video-expanding-to-100.html

22   Media usage in an internet minute as of August 2020 https://www.statista.com/statistics/195140/new-user-generated-content-uploaded-by-users-per-minute/

23   Media usage in an internet minute as of August 2020 https://www.statista.com/statistics/195140/new-user-generated-content-uploaded-by-users-per-minute/

24   State of Video Marketing Survey 2020: The Results Are In! https://www.wyzowl.com/video-marketing-survey-2020/

25   The latest video trends: Where your audience is watching https://www.thinkwithgoogle.com/marketing-strategies/video/video-trends-where-audience-watching/

26   YouTube Video Data Watching Habits https://www.thinkwithgoogle.com/feature/youtube-video-data-watching-habits/#/

27   The Evolution of Online Video: How CPG Marketers Can Harness 4 Key Shifts https://www.facebook.com/business/news/insights/the-evolution-of-online-video-how-cpg-marketers-can-harness-4-key-shifts

28   The Evolution of Online Video: How CPG Marketers Can Harness 4 Key Shifts https://www.facebook.com/business/news/insights/the-evolution-of-online-video-how-cpg-marketers-can-harness-4-key-shifts

29   Top U.S. Online Video Content Properties Ranked by Unique Video Viewers February 2021 https://www.comscore.com/Insights/Rankings#tab_video_top_properties/

30   YouTube At A Crossroads: Social Media Network Or Streaming Service? https://www.ignitesocialmedia.com/youtube-marketing/youtube-at-a-crossroads-social-media-network-or-streaming-service/

31   YouTubers: How YouTube Shook Up T.V. and Created a New Generation of Stars, by Chris Stokel-Walker (Canbury Press, 2019)

32   YouTubers: How YouTube Shook Up T.V. and Created a New Generation of Stars, by Chris Stokel-Walker (Canbury Press, 2019)

33   Facebook Video Ads: The Guide Marketers Are Looking For (Strategies Included) https://adespresso.com/blog/facebook-video-ads-guide/

34   Winning the Attention War: Consumers in Nine Major Markets Now Spend More than Four Hours a Day in Apps https://www.appannie.com/en/insights/market-data/q1-2021-market-index

35 Why TikTok is important https://www.garyvaynerchuk.com/why-tiktok-formerly-musical-ly-app-is-important/

36 Special Feature: YouTube's Evolution in the OTT Streaming Landscape https://www.comscore.com/Insights/Blog/Special-Feature-YouTubes-Evolution-in-the-OTT-Streaming-Landscape

37 How the streaming boom has landed us back in the living room https://www.thinkwithgoogle.com/marketing-resources/streaming-video-trends-for-advertisers/

38 5 things you need to know about the acceleration of the video streaming wars https://www.thinkwithgoogle.com/consumer-insights/video-streaming-wars/
New video research shows what viewers value during the pandemic and beyond https://www.thinkwithgoogle.com/consumer-insights/consumer-trends/pandemic-video-behavior-research-trends/

39 TOPS OF 2020: NIELSEN STREAMING UNWRAPPED https://www.nielsen.com/us/en/insights/article/2021/tops-of-2020-nielsen-streaming-unwrapped/

40 HOW STREAMING ENABLEMENT IN 2020 HAS CHANGED THE MEDIA LANDSCAPE https://www.nielsen.com/us/en/insights/article/2020/how-streaming-enablement-in-2020-has-changed-the-media-landscape/

41 Twitch Streams 1.1 Billion Hours of Content in March, Hitting Record High https://ca.news.yahoo.com/twitch-streams-1-1-billion-184754294.html

42 Twitch breaks records again in Q2, topping 5B total hours watched https://techcrunch.com/2020/07/01/twitch-breaks-records-again-in-q2-topping-5b-total-hours-watched/

43 eMarketer, U.S., U.S. Connected T.V. Households and Penetration Forecasts, Feb. 2021. https://www.emarketer.com/forecasts/

44 *YouTubers: How YouTube Shook Up T.V. and Created a New Generation of Stars,* by Chris Stokel-Walker (Canbury Press, 2019)

45 *The State of Online Video 2020, a report commissioned by Limelight Networks, Inc. to understand consumer perceptions and behaviors around online video.* https://www.limelight.com/resources/market-research/state-of-online-video-2020/

46 *The 2021 VIDYARD Video Benchmark Report* https://www.vidyard.com/business-video-benchmarks/

47 Google Trending Data Shorts: "Why We're Feeling Digital Video" https://www.thinkwithgoogle.com/consumer-insights/consumer-trends/trending-data-shorts/digital-video-streaming-data

48 A Marketer's Guide to Using User-Generated Content on Social Media https://blog.hootsuite.com/user-generated-content-ugc/

49 *The Content Fuel Framework: How to Generate Unlimited Story Ideas (For Marketers and Creators),* by Melanie Deziel

50 *Ofcom Online Nation 2019 Report* https://www.ofcom.org.uk/__data/assets/pdf_file/0024/149253/online-nation-summary.pdf

51 *The 2021 VIDYARD Video Benchmark Report* https://www.vidyard.com/business-video-benchmarks/

52 *The 2021 VIDYARD Video Benchmark Report* https://www.vidyard.com/business-video-benchmarks/

53 More Than 500 Hours Of Content Are Now Being Uploaded To YouTube Every Minute https://www.tubefilter.com/2019/05/07/number-hours-video-uploaded-to-youtube-per-minute/

54   TikTok Statistics – Updated February 2021 https://wallaroomedia.com/blog/social-media/tiktok-statistics/

55   *The 2021 VIDYARD Video Benchmark Report* https://www.vidyard.com/business-video-benchmarks/

56   Mobile and tablet internet usage exceeds desktop for first time worldwide https://gs.statcounter.com/press/mobile-and-tablet-internet-usage-exceeds-desktop-for-first-time-worldwide

57   Shifts for 2020: Multisensory Multipliers https://www.facebook.com/business/news/insights/shifts-for-2020-multisensory-multipliers

58   YouTube press release, sourced from https://www.youtube.com/intl/en-GB/about/press/

59   You'll Spend Almost 9 Years of Your Life Staring at Your Phone https://www.whistleout.com/CellPhones/Guides/5-ways-to-limit-screentime-at-bedtime#screentime

60   eMarketer, Global Digital Video 2019 https://www.emarketer.com/content/digital-video-2019

61   YouTube Internal Data, Global, June 2020

62   *The 2021 VIDYARD Video Benchmark Report* https://www.vidyard.com/business-video-benchmarks/

63   *Ericsson Mobility Report 2020* https://www.ericsson.com/49da93/assets/local/mobility-report/documents/2020/june2020-ericsson-mobility-report.pdf

64   *State of Mobile, by App Annie* https://www.appannie.com/en/go/state-of-mobile-2021/

65   Ofcom Online Nation 2020 U.K. Report *https://www.ofcom.org.uk/research-and-data/internet-and-on-demand-research/online-nation*

66   What the world watched in a day https://www.thinkwithgoogle.com/feature/youtube-video-data-watching-habits/#/

67   What the world watched in a day https://www.thinkwithgoogle.com/feature/youtube-video-data-watching-habits/#/

68   What the world watched in a day https://www.thinkwithgoogle.com/feature/youtube-video-data-watching-habits/#/

69   Live Streaming Statistics https://techjury.net/blog/live-streaming-statistics/#gref

70   Live Streaming Statistics https://techjury.net/blog/live-streaming-statistics/#gref

71   Live Streaming Statistics https://techjury.net/blog/live-streaming-statistics/#gref

72   State of Video Marketing Survey 2020: The Results Are In! https://www.wyzowl.com/video-marketing-survey-2020/

73   *The Power of Visual Storytelling: How to Use Visuals, Videos, and Social Media to Market Your Brand*, by Ekaterina Walter, Jessica Gioglio

74   Design Psychology: 10 Essential Experimental Principles https://inkbotdesign.medium.com/design-psychology-10-essential-experimental-principles-6e52f8162772

75   *YouTube Secrets: The Ultimate Guide to Growing Your Following and Making Money as a Video Influencer*, by Sean Cannell and Benji Travis

76   *YouTube Secrets: The Ultimate Guide to Growing Your Following and Making Money as a Video Influencer*, by Sean Cannell and Benji Travis

77   *YouTubers: How YouTube Shook Up T.V. and Created a New Generation of Stars*, by Chris Stokel-Walker (Canbury Press, 2019)

78   *TikTok Marketing for Viral Sales: A Young Girl's Guide to Blowing Customers' Minds*, by Anastasia Olson

79 How to create an effective video ad for every stage of the customer journey https://www.thinkwithgoogle.com/future-of-marketing/creativity/youtube-video-ad-creative/

80 *Video Marketing Strategy: Harness the Power of Online Video to Drive Brand Growth*, by Jon Mowat

81 *Hook Point: How to Stand Out in a 3 Second World*, by Brendan Kane (Waterside Productions, 2020)

82 COVID-19 CHANGED THE ADVERTISING PLAYBOOK. NOW WHAT? https://www.nielsen.com/us/en/insights/article/2021/covid-19-changed-the-advertising-playbook-now-what/

83 Video ad spend bucks H1 digital dip https://www.warc.com/newsandopinion/news/video-ads-pend-bucks-h1-digital-dip/44234

84 Online video and social advertising to accelerate this year https://www.warc.com/content/paywall/article/warc-datapoints/online-video-and-social-advertising-to-accelerate-this-year/136319

85 State of Video Marketing Survey 2020: The Results Are In! https://www.wyzowl.com/video-marketing-survey-2020/

86 *Nielsen Annual Marketing Report: The Era of Adaptation (2021)* https://content.nielsen.com/2021/report/amr/pr

87 Video marketing statistics to know for 2020 https://www.smartinsights.com/digital-marketing-platforms/video-marketing/video-marketing-statistics-to-know/

88 *The 2021 VIDYARD Video Benchmark Report* https://www.vidyard.com/business-video-benchmarks/

89 *The 2021 VIDYARD Video Benchmark Report* https://www.vidyard.com/business-video-benchmarks/

90 *The 2021 VIDYARD Video Benchmark Report* https://www.vidyard.com/business-video-benchmarks/

91 Social Video Trends: What Marketers Say vs. What They Do [Infographic] https://animoto.com/blog/industry-news/social-video-trends-marketers-say-vs-do-infographic/

92 Video Streaming Market Worth USD 70.05 Billion by 2021 - Online Video Streaming has Increased Viewership 60% - Research and Markets https://www.prnewswire.com/news-releases/video-streaming-market-worth-usd-7005-billion-by-2021---online-video-streaming-has-increased-viewership-60---research-and-markets-300267717.html

93 *The 2021 VIDYARD Video Benchmark Report* https://www.vidyard.com/business-video-benchmarks/

94 United Kingdom Jobs on the Rise https://business.linkedin.com/talent-solutions/resources/talent-acquisition/jobs-on-the-rise-uk-cont-fact

95 *Digital Marketing like a PRO,* by Clo Willaerts (2018)

96 Maslow's Hierarchy of Needs | Simply Psychology https://www.simplypsychology.org/maslow.html

97 *Get Together: How to Build a Community with Your People, by Bailey Richardson, Kai Elmer Sotto, and Kevin Huynh (2019)*

98 *Tools of Titans,* by Tim Ferriss (2016)

99 *The Infinite Game,* by Simon Sinek

100 "Money for Nothing," a song by British rock band Dire Straits, is the second track on their fifth studio album, *Brothers in Arms (1985).*

101 Viral Video https://en.wikipedia.org/wiki/Viral_video

102 Creating Online Videos That Engage Viewers https://sloanreview.mit.edu/article/creating-online-videos-that-engage-viewers/

103   *Digital Marketing Like a PRO*, by Clo Willaerts

104   Anthony Quintano from Hillsborough, NJ, United States - Mission Accomplished - ALS Ice Bucket Challenge See the video here: youtu.be/lRicUkYwDpE Used a GoPro to have the perspective from inside the bucket. Photo taken by my wife Kim Quintano. See her photography here: www.flickr.com/photos/kimberlyquintano/

105   TikTok Growth Hacks for Viral Success https://bettermarketing.pub/tiktok-growth-hacks-for-viral-success-29d6a4fb7414

106   *Video Smart: Make smartphone videos like a pro,* by Pelpina Trip

107   *Video Marketing Strategy: Harness the Power of Online Video to Drive Brand Growth*, by Jon Mowat (2018)

108   Building a brand in an age of hyper-targeted messaging https://www.thinkwithgoogle.com/intl/en-154/marketing-strategies/video/branding-video-advertising/

109   *YouTube for Business: Online Video Marketing for Any Business*, by Michael Miller (2018)

110   *Hook Point: How to Stand Out in a 3-Second World*, by Brendan Kane (Waterside Productions, 2020)

111   *Hook Point: How to Stand Out in a 3-Second World*, by Brendan Kane (Waterside Productions, 2020)

112   A B C D, A playbook for building effective creative on YouTube https://www.thinkwithgoogle.com/_qs/documents/8472/ABCD_Complete_V7b_HR_1.pdf

113   *Hook Point: How to Stand Out in a 3-Second World*, by Brendan Kane (2020)

114   *YouTubers: How YouTube Shook Up TV and Created a New Generation of Stars, by Chris Stokel-Walker (Canbury Press, 2019)*

115   *Video Marketing for Beginners: Simple Easy Video Solution*, by Joshua Samuel (2020)

116   YouTube Creator Academy Ad Promotion https://creatoracademy.youtube.com/page/lesson/ad-promotion

117   Best practices for video campaigns https://www.youtube.com/intl/en_us/ads/resources/best-practices/

118   YouTube Re:View Newsletter https://getsubscriptions.withgoogle.com/newsletter/signup/landing/

119   YouTube Ads Leaderboard https://www.youtube.com/intl/en_us/ads/news-and-inspiration/ads-leaderboard/

120   YouTube success stories https://www.youtube.com/intl/en_us/ads/resources/success-stories/

121   Google Ads Video Certification https://skillshop.exceedlms.com/student/path/18216-google-ads-video-certification

122   YouTube success stories https://www.youtube.com/intl/en_us/ads/resources/success-stories/

123   YouTube Advertising News and inspiration https://www.youtube.com/intl/en_us/ads/news-and-inspiration/

124   Get inspiration from the YouTube Works Award winners: https://www.youtube.com/ads/youtube-works/

125   TikTok For Business Creative Center (TikTok for Business) https://ads.tiktok.com/business/creativecenter/en

126   TikTok Blog: Updates, insights, and creative inspiration from our vibrant business community on TikTok. https://www.tiktok.com/business/en/blog

127   TikTok For Business Small Business Resource Center https://www.tiktok.com/business/en/smb-center

[128]   9 creative tips to drive performance https://ads.tiktok.com/business/creativecenter/insight/deta il?articleId=6867427865592332294

[129]   Facebook Video Ad Specs for Instagram Feed, Video Views (Facebook for Business) https://www. facebook.com/business/ads-guide/video/instagram-feed/video-views

[130]   Create Engaging Instagram Ads https://www.facebook.com/business/learn/lessons/create-en-gaging-instagram-ads

[131]   Facebook IQ articles about video ads on Instagram https://www.facebook.com/business/news/in sights?tags[0]=instagram&tags[1]=video

[132]   Twitch Premium Video https://twitchadvertising.tv/ad-products/twitch-premium-video/

[133]   Twitch Ads: How They Work and How to Run Them https://influencermarketinghub.com/twitch-ads/

[134]   Facebook Video Ad Format https://www.facebook.com/business/ads/video-ad-format

[135]   Facebook Blueprint tutorials https://www.facebookblueprint.com/

[136]   The essential guide to finding visuals for your ads (Facebook Blueprint Course) https://www.face-book.com/business/learn/lessons/how-to-create-a-video-for-your-facebook-ad

[137]   Facebook Business Help Center about Video Ads https://www.facebook.com/business/help/1381 779698788633?id=603833089963720

[138]   The Fundamental Strategies for Video Ads on LinkedIn: A Guide to High-Performing Creative https://business.linkedin.com/marketing-solutions/native-advertising/video-ads/video-ads-best-practices

[139]   LinkedIn Video Ads Best Practices https://business.linkedin.com/marketing-solutions/native-advertising/video-ads/video-ads-best-practices

[140]   The Fundamental Strategies of Video Ads on LinkedIn (LinkedIn Marketing Solutions) https:// business.linkedin.com/content/dam/me/business/en-us/amp/marketing-solutions/pdf/NA-MER_Video-Ads-Playbook-v02-03.pdf

[141]   Pinterest Business creator newsletter Be the first to hear about product launches, emerging trends, and inspiring content ideas. https://business.pinterest.com/creator-newsletter/

[142]   *Hook Point: How to Stand Out in a 3-Second World,* by Brendan Kane (Waterside Productions, 2020)

[143]   YouTube Creator Academy https://creatoracademy.youtube.com/page/lesson/brand-identity

[144]   *YouTube Secrets: The Ultimate Guide to Growing Your Following and Making Money as a Video Influencer* by Sean Cannell and Benji Travis (Lioncrest Publishing, 2018)

[145]   *Your Music and People*, by Derek Sivers (Sound Foundation, 2020)

[146]   Decoding how consumers make purchase decisions https://www.thinkwithgoogle.com/intl/en-aunz/consumer-insights/consumer-journey/decoding-how-consumers-make-purchase-decisi-ons/

[147]   How people decide what to buy lies in the "messy middle" of the purchase journey https://www. thinkwithgoogle.com/intl/en-154/consumer-insights/consumer-journey/navigating-purchase-behavior-and-decision-making/

[148]   *Your Music and People*, by Derek Sivers ((Sound Foundation, 2020)

[149]   Hiking and camping equipment by Decathlon https://www.quechua.com/quechua-hiking-and-camping-equipment-by-decathlon

[150]   How To Add a Google My Business Video: Guidelines, Ideas, Best Practices https://blog.wave.vi-deo/blog/google-my-business-video/

151   How to Make a Good Video for Google My Business https://gmbgorilla.com/how-to-make-a-good-video-for-google-my-business/

152   *YouTubers: How YouTube Shook Up TV and Created a New Generation of Stars,* by Chris Stokel-Walker (Canbury Press, 2019)

153   Haul Video https://en.wikipedia.org/wiki/Haul_video

154   How to Make the Best Unboxing Videos – GUIDE https://www.expertvoice.com/unboxing-videos-guide/

155   *TikTok Marketing for Viral Sales: A Young Girl's Guide to Blowing Customers' Minds,* by Anastasia Olson (Book2Climb LLC, 2020)

156   Using Video and Email Together https://wistia.com/learn/marketing/using-video-in-email

157   Displaying Video in Clients That Support Video iOS 10 and above https://www.emailonacid.com/blog/article/email-development/a_how_to_guide_to_embedding_html5_video_in_email/

158   How to Use Video in Your Email Marketing https://www.campaignmonitor.com/resources/guides/video-in-email/

159   How to Create Video Landing Pages That Convert https://www.vidyard.com/blog/video-landing-pages/

160   The Benefits of Using Video on Landing Pages https://unbounce.com/landing-page-articles/the-benefits-of-using-video-on-landing-pages/

161   How to Create Video Landing Pages That Convert https://www.vidyard.com/blog/video-landing-pages/

162   US eCommerce grows 44.0% in 2020 https://www.digitalcommerce360.com/article/us-ecommerce-sales/

163   2019 State Of Video & Interactive Content https://www.demandgenreport.com/resources/reports/2019-state-of-video-interactive-content/

164   How to Create Shoppable Videos That Convert! https://www.channelsight.com/blog/shoppable-video-the-rising-star-of-your-marketing-strategy

165   Drive results with new direct response solutions on YouTube https://www.blog.google/products/ads/new-ways-to-drive-action/

166   Set Up TikTok Conversion Ads on Shopify https://ads.tiktok.com/help/article?aid=10001357

167   A Comprehensive Guide to Live Stream Shopping https://influencermarketinghub.com/live-stream-shopping/

168   Quoted in: The Evolution of Online Video: How CPG Marketers Can Harness 4 Key Shifts https://www.facebook.com/business/news/insights/the-evolution-of-online-video-how-cpg-marketers-can-harness-4-key-shifts

169   Digital Commerce 360 analysis of US Department of Commerce data, updated Jan. 2021, https://www.thinkwithgoogle.com/marketing-strategies/video/post-pandemic-video-trends/

170   Gen-Z and the future of Livestream shopping https://www.thedrum.com/opinion/2021/04/13/gen-z-and-the-future-livestream-shopping

171   6 reasons why customer satisfaction is important https://www.allaboutcalls.co.uk/the-call-takers-blog/6-reasons-why-customer-satisfaction-is-important

172   5 Ways to Turn Your Unhappy Customer into a Valuable Resource https://neilpatel.com/blog/unhappy-customers-into-resource/ (2017)

173   Spend time collecting enough data to get a reasonably reliable picture of your customer loyalty https://www.nicereply.com/blog/the-importance-of-customer-loyalty/

174   3 Customer Retention Strategies using Video – Customer Success Managers Edition https://clip-champ.com/en/blog/video-marketing-customer-retention-strategies/

175   How to Use Video for Support to Improve Customer Satisfaction https://www.vidyard.com/blog/video-customer-support/

176   Why Brand Advocacy Is The Holy Grail Of Marketing Today https://scholarlyoa.com/brand-advocacy-is-holy-grail-of-marketing/

177   *The Content Fuel Framework: How to Generate Unlimited Story Ideas (For Marketers and Creators)*, by Melanie Deziel (StoryFuel Press, 2020)

178   *The Content Fuel Framework: How to Generate Unlimited Story Ideas (For Marketers and Creators)*, by Melanie Deziel (StoryFuel Press, 2020)

179   *Your Music and People*, by Derek Sivers (Sound Foundation, 2020)

180   *YouTube Secrets: The Ultimate Guide to Growing Your Following and Making Money as a Video Influencer*, by Sean Cannell and Benji Travis

181   *YouTube Secrets: The Ultimate Guide to Growing Your Following and Making Money as a Video Influencer*, by Sean Cannell and Benji Travis

182   *The Content Fuel Framework: How to Generate Unlimited Story Ideas (For Marketers and Creators)*, by Melanie Deziel (StoryFuel Press, 2020)

183   Why You Need to Rethink the Talking-Head Video: 4 Tips to Improve Engagement https://tendo-com.com/blog/why-you-need-to-rethink-the-talking-head-web-video/

184   *YouTubers: How YouTube Shook Up TV and Created a New Generation of Stars*, by Chris Stokel-Walker (Canbury Press, 2019)

185   What is a native video? (And how it can get you more views!) https://biteable.com/blog/what-is-native-video/

186   The Apollo Theater, Still Performing Live With Video https://vimeo.com/blog/post/apollo-thea-ter-live-video-vimeo/

187   The Marketer's Guide to Live Streaming https://wistia.com/learn/marketing/how-to-set-yourself-up-for-livestreaming-success

188   What is Multistreaming? https://streamyard.com/resources/what-is-multistreaming/

189   YouTube Digital Events Playbook https://www.youtube.com/intl/en_be/howyoutubeworks/pro-duct-features/live/

190   Creator Academy Learning Toolkits. Learn the basics of getting started with Live Streaming and best practices, including features and setup tips, that can help you take your next Live Stream to the next level. https://creatoracademy.youtube.com/page/learning-toolkits

191   Facebook For Media Tips for using Facebook Live https://www.facebook.com/formedia/blog/tips-for-using-live

192   What is Aspect Ratio? https://wistia.com/learn/production/what-is-aspect-ratio

193   The Complete Instagram Video Size Guide for 2021(+6 Video Tools to Try) https://influencermar-ketinghub.com/instagram-video-size/

194   *YouTubers: How YouTube Shook Up TV and Created a New Generation of Stars*, by Chris Stokel-Walker (Canbury Press, 2019)

195   *The essential guide to finding visuals for your ads (Facebook Blueprint Course) https://www.facebook.com/business/learn/lessons/how-to-create-a-video-for-your-facebook-ad*

196   *YouTube for Business: Online Video Marketing for Any Business*, by Michael Miller (Que Publishing)

197   *Video Smart: Make smartphone videos like a pro, by Pelpina Trip (Pelpina Publishing, 2020)*

198   *YouTubers: How YouTube Shook Up TV and Created a New Generation of Stars*, by Chris Stokel-Walker (Canbury Press, 2019)

199   *TikTok Marketing for Viral Sales: A Young Girl's Guide to Blowing Customers' Minds,* by Anastasia Olson (Book2Climb LLC, 2020)

200   *YouTubers: How YouTube Shook Up TV and Created a New Generation of Stars, by Chris Stokel-Walker (Canbury Press, 2019)*

201   Using Video for Instagram https://business.instagram.com/blog/using-video-on-instagram

202   Ultimate Guide to Instagram Video: Stories, IGTV, Live, Posts, & More! https://later.com/blog/instagram-video/

203   Instagram Video: A Complete Guide https://animoto.com/blog/guides/instagram-video

204   Instagram Video: Best Practices and Tools for Creating Engaging Content (Hootsuite, 2021) https://blog.hootsuite.com/instagram-video/

205   The Ultimate Guide to Instagram for Businesses in 2021 https://www.oberlo.com/blog/instagram-video

206   CMA Online platforms and digital advertising market study: final report https://www.iabuk.com/policy/cma-online-platforms-and-digital-advertising-market-study-final-report

207   Facebook for Business: How to make a video for Facebook https://www.facebook.com/business/m/how-to-create-videos

208   Facebook For Business – Business Help Center: About Video https://www.facebook.com/business/help/487054428419936?id=214359809769375

209   Facebook Blueprint Course: Your Video Best Practices Checklist https://www.facebook.com/business/learn/lessons/video-best-practices-checklist

210   Facebook for Media: Understanding How Your Videos Perform on Facebook https://www.facebook.com/formedia/blog/understanding-how-your-videos-perform-on-facebook

211   *Attention Factory: The Story of TikTok and China's ByteDance,* by Matthew Brennan

212   *20/20 Vision for Mobile Video Outlook for a new era of mobile-first experiences, by The National Research Group, commissioned by Snap Inc.* https://forbusiness.snapchat.com/blog/us-2020-vision-for-mobile-video

213   Twitter: About Our Company https://about.twitter.com/en/who-we-are/our-company

214   What were they thinking? No, really.

215   LinkedIn Marketing Solutions: Video Ads https://business.linkedin.com/marketing-solutions/native-advertising/video-ads

216   Everything You Need to Know About LinkedIn Video (Hootsuite, 2021) https://blog.hootsuite.com/linkedin-video/

217   All About Pinterest https://help.pinterest.com/en/guide/all-about-pinterest

218   *Video Marketing Strategy: Harness the Power of Online Video to Drive Brand Growth,* by Jon Mowat (Kogan Page, 2018)

219   *Video Marketing Strategy: Harness the Power of Online Video to Drive Brand Growth,* by Jon Mowat (Kogan Page, 2018)

220   YouTube Creator Academy https://creatoracademy.youtube.com/page/lesson/trendsetter?hl=en

221   *Vlog Like a Boss: How to Kill It Online with Video Blogging,* by Amy Schmittauer (Author Academy Elite, 2017)

222 *Vlog Like a Boss: How to Kill It Online with Video Blogging,* by Amy Schmittauer (Author Academy Elite, 2017)

223 *The Content Fuel Framework: How to Generate Unlimited Story Ideas (For Marketers and Creators),* by Melanie Deziel (StoryFuel Press, 2020)

224 *Video Marketing in 2019 Made (Stupidly) Easy: How to Achieve YouTube Business Awesomeness,* by Michael Clarke (Punk Rock Marketing)

225 *The Filmmaker's Handbook: A Comprehensive Guide for the Digital Age: Fifth Edition,* by Steven Ascher & Edward Pincus (Plume, 2019)

226 *The Filmmaker's Handbook: A Comprehensive Guide for the Digital Age: Fifth Edition,* by Steven Ascher & Edward Pincus (Plume, 2019)

227 Learn about building your team and other business skills at YouTube Creator Academy https://creatoracademy.youtube.com/page/lesson/building-team?cid=business-skills&hl=en

228 *Video Marketing in 2019 Made (Stupidly) Easy: How to Achieve YouTube Business Awesomeness,* by Michael Clarke (Punk Rock Marketing)

229 *The Filmmaker's Handbook: A Comprehensive Guide for the Digital Age: Fifth Edition,* by Steven Ascher & Edward Pincus (Plume, 2019)

230 *The Filmmaker's Handbook: A Comprehensive Guide for the Digital Age: Fifth Edition,* by Steven Ascher & Edward Pincus (Plume, 2019)

231 Wistia: Choosing a Background for Your Video https://wistia.com/learn/production/choosing-a-background

232 *The Filmmaker's Handbook: A Comprehensive Guide for the Digital Age: Fifth Edition,* by Steven Ascher & Edward Pincus (Plume, 2019)

233 *Vlog Like a Boss: How to Kill It Online with Video Blogging,* by Amy Schmittauer (Author Academy Elite, 2017)

234 Wistia: The Down and Dirty DIY Lighting Kit https://wistia.com/learn/production/down-and-dirty-lighting-kit

235 *The Filmmaker's Handbook: A Comprehensive Guide for the Digital Age: Fifth Edition,* by Steven Ascher & Edward Pincus (Plume, 2019)

236 *TikTok Marketing for Viral Sales: A Young Girl's Guide to Blowing Customers' Minds,* by Anastasia Olson (Book2Climb LLC, 2020)

237 *The Filmmaker's Handbook: A Comprehensive Guide for the Digital Age: Fifth Edition,* by Steven Ascher & Edward Pincus (Plume, 2019)

238 *TikTok Marketing for Viral Sales: A Young Girl's Guide to Blowing Customers' Minds,* by Anastasia Olson (Book2Climb LLC, 2020)

239 *TikTok Marketing for Viral Sales: A Young Girl's Guide to Blowing Customers' Minds,* by Anastasia Olson (Book2Climb LLC, 2020)

240 *Your Music and People,* by Derek Sivers (Sound Foundation, 2020)

241 *Video Marketing in 2019 Made (Stupidly) Easy: How to Achieve YouTube Business Awesomeness,* by Michael Clarke (Punk Rock Marketing)

242 *Video Marketing in 2019 Made (Stupidly) Easy: How to Achieve YouTube Business Awesomeness,* by Michael Clarke (Punk Rock Marketing)

243 *Vlog Like a Boss: How to Kill It Online with Video Blogging,* by Amy Schmittauer (Author Academy Elite, 2017)

244 *Standout Virtual Events: How to create an experience that your audience will love*, by David Meerman Scott and Michelle Manafy (2020)

245 *Video Smart: Make smartphone videos like a pro*, by Pelpina Trip (Pelpina Publishing, 2020)

246 *YouTube Secrets: The Ultimate Guide to Growing Your Following and Making Money as a Video Influencer*, by Sean Cannell and Benji Travis (Lioncrest Publishing, 2018)

247 *Your Music and People*, by Derek Sivers (Sound Foundation, 2020)

248 *The Filmmaker's Handbook: A Comprehensive Guide for the Digital Age: Fifth Edition*, by Steven Ascher & Edward Pincus (Plume, 2019)

249 Wistia: The Best Way to Shoot a Video by Yourself https://wistia.com/learn/production/shooting-video-by-yourself

250 *YouTube for Business: Online Video Marketing for Any Business*, by Michael Miller (Que Publishing)

251 *YouTube Secrets: The Ultimate Guide to Growing Your Following and Making Money as a Video Influencer*, by Sean Cannell and Benji Travis (Lioncrest Publishing, 2018)

252 *TikTok Marketing for Viral Sales: A Young Girl's Guide to Blowing Customers' Minds*, by Anastasia Olson (Book2Climb LLC, 2020)

253 MKBHD Gear Tour: How to Shoot Videos People Want to Watch (23 March 2021 on Skillshare YouTube channel) https://www.youtube.com/watch?v=EQ9N-2UrZC4

254 *Video Marketing in 2019 Made (Stupidly) Easy: How to Achieve YouTube Business Awesomeness*, by Michael Clarke (Punk Rock Marketing)

255 *The Filmmaker's Handbook: A Comprehensive Guide for the Digital Age: Fifth Edition*, by Steven Ascher & Edward Pincus (Plume, 2019)

256 *The Filmmaker's Handbook: A Comprehensive Guide for the Digital Age: Fifth Edition*, by Steven Ascher & Edward Pincus (Plume, 2019)

257 *The Filmmaker's Handbook: A Comprehensive Guide for the Digital Age: Fifth Edition*, by Steven Ascher & Edward Pincus (Plume, 2019)

258 How Long it Takes Me to Make a YouTube Video https://birchtree.me/blog/how-long-it-takes-me-to-make-a-youtube-video/

259 *How to Shoot Video That Doesn't Suck*, by Steve Stockman (Workman Publishing Company, 2011)

260 *The Filmmaker's Handbook: A Comprehensive Guide for the Digital Age: Fifth Edition*, by Steven Ascher & Edward Pincus (Plume, 2019)

261 *Video Smart: Make smartphone videos like a pro*, by Pelpina Trip (Pelpina Publishing, 2020)

262 Wistia Guide: Editing Basics for Business Video https://wistia.com/learn/production/editing-your-business-video

263 Wistia Guide: Editing Basics for Business Video https://wistia.com/learn/production/editing-your-business-video

264 Wistia Guide: Editing Basics for Business Video https://wistia.com/learn/production/editing-your-business-video

265 Wistia Guide: Editing Basics for Business Video https://wistia.com/learn/production/editing-your-business-video

266 *Video Smart: Make smartphone videos like a pro*, by Pelpina Trip (Pelpina Publishing, 2020)

267 *The Filmmaker's Handbook: A Comprehensive Guide for the Digital Age: Fifth Edition*, by Steven Ascher & Edward Pincus (Plume, 2019)

268 *Vlog Like a Boss: How to Kill It Online with Video Blogging*, by Amy Schmittauer (Author Academy Elite, 2017)

269   GaryVee's Content Model https://www.garyvaynerchuk.com/the-garyvee-content-strategy-how-to-grow-and-distribute-your-brands-social-media-content/

270   *Vlog Like a Boss: How to Kill It Online with Video Blogging,* by Amy Schmittauer (Author Academy Elite, 2017)

271   *Attention Factory: The Story of TikTok and China's ByteDance,* by Matthew Brennan

272   Creator Academy: Advantages of Subscribers https://creatoracademy.youtube.com/page/lesson/subscriber-advantage?cid=bootcamp-foundations&hl=en

273   *Your Music and People,* by Derek Sivers (Sound Foundation, 2020)

274   *Hook Point: How to Stand Out in a 3-Second World,* by Brendan Kane (Waterside Productions, 2020)

275   *Your Music and People,* by Derek Sivers (Sound Foundation, 2020)

276   *YouTube Secrets: The Ultimate Guide to Growing Your Following and Making Money as a Video Influencer,* by Sean Cannell and Benji Travis (Lioncrest Publishing, 2018)

277   *Hook Point: How to Stand Out in a 3-Second World,* by Brendan Kane (Waterside Productions, 2020)

278   Discovery   Algorithm   on   YouTube   https://creatoracademy.youtube.com/page/lesson/discovery?hl=en

279   How is YouTube using AI to recommend videos? https://dakshtrehan.medium.com/how-is-youtube-using-ai-to-recommend-videos-d897e41d5867

280   *Hook Point: How to Stand Out in a 3-Second World,* by Brendan Kane (Waterside Productions, 2020)

281   *Attention Factory: The Story of TikTok and China's ByteDance,* by Matthew Brennan

282   *TikTok Marketing for Viral Sales: A Young Girl's Guide to Blowing Customers' Minds,* by Anastasia Olson (Book2Climb LLC, 2020)

283   YouTube Creator Academy: Discoverability and Analytics https://creatoracademy.youtube.com/page/lesson/discoverability-analytics?hl=en

284   5 Super Annoying Types of YouTube Clickbait https://bettermarketing.pub/5-super-annoying-types-of-youtube-clickbait-a701760650b

285   YouTube SEO https://biteable.com/blog/youtube-seo/

286   *YouTube Secrets: The Ultimate Guide to Growing Your Following and Making Money as a Video Influencer,* by Sean Cannell and Benji Travis (Lioncrest Publishing, 2018)

287   *Video Marketing in 2019 Made (Stupidly) Easy: How to Achieve YouTube Business Awesomeness,* by Michael Clarke (Punk Rock Marketing)

288   The 17 Best Places Ecommerce Entrepreneurs Go to Find Product Ideas https://www.shopify.com/blog/product-ideas

289   The 17 Best Places Ecommerce Entrepreneurs Go to Find Product Ideas https://www.shopify.com/blog/product-ideas

290   The 17 Best Places Ecommerce Entrepreneurs Go to Find Product Ideas https://www.shopify.com/blog/product-ideas

291   Google   Trends   for   Google   Shopping   https://trends.google.com/trends/explore?gprop=froogle

292   Video Monetization: How To Make Money Without YouTube https://www.uscreen.tv/blog/video-monetization-without-youtube/

293   YouTube Creator Academy: Monetization https://creatoracademy.youtube.com/page/learning-toolkits/?hl=en#monetization

294   The state of ad viewability https://www.thinkwithgoogle.com/feature/viewability/state-of-viewability/

295   Alejandro Rioja Highest CPC Keywords and Best Adsense Niches https://alejandrorioja.com/high-cpc-adsense-keywords/

296   About Video Content Eligible for Monetization https://www.facebook.com/business/help/24367 8566401546?id=1200580480150259

297   Brand Collabs Manager https://www.facebook.com/creators/tools/brand-collabs-manager

298   *Attention Factory: The Story of TikTok and China's ByteDance,* by Matthew Brennan

299   Introducing the YouTube Shorts Fund https://blog.youtube/news-and-events/introducing-youtube-shorts-fund/

300   Six Ways New Social Companies Will Monetize https://a16z.com/2020/12/07/social-strikes-back-after-ads/

301   *YouTube Secrets: The Ultimate Guide to Growing Your Following and Making Money as a Video Influencer,* by Sean Cannell and Benji Travis (Lioncrest Publishing, 2018)

302   Six Ways New Social Companies Will Monetize https://a16z.com/2020/12/07/social-strikes-back-after-ads/

303   Facebook Blueprint Course Earn money with your live video with Stars https://www.facebook.com/business/learn/lessons/how-to-make-money-with-facebook-stars

304   *YouTubers: How YouTube Shook Up TV and Created a New Generation of Stars,* by Chris Stokel-Walker (Canbury Press, 2019)

305   Six Ways New Social Companies Will Monetize https://a16z.com/2020/12/07/social-strikes-back-after-ads/

306   YouTube Creator Academy: Grow your community https://creatoracademy.youtube.com/page/course/fans?hl=en

307   Six Ways New Social Companies Will Monetize https://a16z.com/2020/12/07/social-strikes-back-after-ads/

308   Six Ways New Social Companies Will Monetize https://a16z.com/2020/12/07/social-strikes-back-after-ads/

309   *YouTubers: How YouTube Shook Up TV and Created a New Generation of Stars,* by Chris Stokel-Walker (Canbury Press, 2019)

310   Youtube channel finances 2019 (41K subs) https://www.reddit.com/r/dataisbeautiful/comments/eulmi6/oc_youtube_channel_finances_2019_41k_subs/

311   *TikTok Marketing for Viral Sales: A Young Girl's Guide to Blowing Customers' Minds,* by Anastasia Olson (Book2Climb LLC, 2020)

312   Productivity Game YouTube Channel https://www.youtube.com/channel/UC02x9yG9ZFF_VZp-1VnMoptg and website http://www.productivitygame.com

313   Six Ways New Social Companies Will Monetize https://a16z.com/2020/12/07/social-strikes-back-after-ads/

314   Gage Skidmore https://www.flickr.com/photos/gageskidmore/14571873893

315   15 Best Video Production Companies to Share Your Message in 2021 https://influencermarketinghub.com/video-production-companies/

316   How to make money with videos https://vimeo.com/blog/post/how-to-monetize-videos/

317   Ready, set, sell! How to sell streaming videos online https://vimeo.com/blog/post/how-to-sell-streaming-videos-online/